He Is Altogether Lovely

Sermons from the Song of Solomon
Delivered by C. H. Spurgeon

TABLE OF CONTENTS

Praise for **_He Is Altogether Lovely_**

"The Prince of Preachers is at his best when extolling the beauties and glories of our lovely Savior. This is very conspicuous in this wonderful collection of sermons by the great Spurgeon taken from his messages from "Song of Solomon," or "Canticles," as often referred to by the Puritans.

The loveliness of God's Son is an ocean that can never be exhausted, but it is one in which we can bathe our souls to their eternal delight. Let this book be a warm bath for your soul. It is a glorious portrait of He who is 'altogether lovely.'"

Dr. Don Kistler
Founder, Soli Deo Gloria and
The Northampton Press

THE BEST BELOVED

DELIVERED BY C. H. SPURGEON
AT THE METROPOLITAN TABERNACLE,
NEWINGTON.

"...yea, he is altogether lovely."

Song of Solomon 5:16

No words can ever express the gratitude we owe to Him who loved us even when we were dead in trespasses and sins! The love of Jesus is unutterably precious and worthy of daily praise. No songs can ever fitly celebrate the triumphs of that salvation which He worked single-handedly on our behalf—the work of Jesus is glorious beyond comparison and all the harps of angels fall short of its worthy honor. Yet I believe and my heart prompts me to say so, that the highest praise of every ransomed soul and of the entire Christian Church should be offered to the blessed *Person* of Jesus Christ, our adorable Lord. The love of His heart is excelled by the heart which gave forth that love; and the wonders of His hands are outdone by the hands themselves, which worked those Divine miracles of Grace.

We ought to bless Him for what He has done for us as Mediator in the place of humble service under the Law and for what He suffered for us as Substitute on the altar of sacrifice from before the foundation of the world—and for what He is doing for us as Advocate in the place of highest honor at the right hand of the Majesty on high! But still, the best thing about Christ is Christ Himself! We prize Him, but we worship Him! His gifts are valued, but He, Himself, is adored! While we contemplate, with mingled feelings of awe, admiration and thankfulness, His Atonement, His Resurrection, His Glory in Heaven and His Second Coming, still, it is Christ, Himself, stupendous in His dignity as the Son of God and superbly beautiful as the Son of Man who sheds an incomparable charm on all those wonderful achievements wherein His might and His merit, His goodness and His Grace appear so conspicuous!

For Him let our choicest spices be reserved and to Him let our sweetest anthems be raised. Our choicest ointment must be poured upon His head and for Him alone, our most costly alabaster boxes must be broken. "He is altogether lovely." Not only is His teaching attractive, His doctrine persuasive, His life irreproachable, His Character enchanting, and His work a self-denying labor for the common good of all His people, but He, Himself, is altogether lovely! I suppose at first we shall always begin to love Him because He first loved us and even to the last His love to us will always be the strongest motive of our affection towards Him. But there ought to be added to this another reason less connected with *ourselves* and more entirely arising out of His own superlative excellence—we ought to love Him because He is lovely and deserves to be loved!

The time should come and with some of us it *has* come, when we can heartily say, "We love Him because we cannot help it, for His all-conquering loveliness has quite ravished our hearts." Surely it is but an unripe fruit to love Him merely for the benefits which we have received at His hands. It is a fruit of Grace, but it is not of the ripest flavor. There are other fruits, both new and old, which we have laid up for You, O our Beloved, and some of them have a daintier taste. There is a sweet and mellow fruit which can only be brought forth by the summer sun of fellowship—love because of the Redeemer's intrinsic goodness and personal sweetness. Oh that we might love our Lord for His own sake! Love Him because He is so supremely beautiful that a glimpse of Him has won our hearts and made Him dearer to our eyes than light! Oh that all true and faithful disciples of our beloved Lord would press forward towards that state of affection and never rest till they reach it!

If any of you have not reached it, you need not, therefore, doubt your own safety, for whatever the reason why you love Jesus—if you love Him at all—it is a sure pledge and token that He loves you and that you are saved in Him with an everlasting salvation! Still, covet earnestly the best gifts and rise to the highest degree of devotion. Love as the purest of the saints have loved! Love as John the Apostle loved, for your Lord exceeds all the loving homage you can pay to Him. Love His Person. Love Him for He is better than all that He has done or given! And as from Himself all blessings flow, so back to Himself should all love return!

Our text tells us that Christ is altogether lovely. What a wealth of thought and feeling is contained in that exclamation! I am embarrassed to know how to preach on such a subject and half inclined to wish it had not been laid so much upon my heart. What, I pray you, what is loveliness? To discern it is one thing, but it is quite another thing to *describe* it! There is not one among us but knows how to appreciate beauty and to be enamored by its attractions. But how many here could tell us what it is? Stand up, my Brother, and define it! Perhaps while you were sitting down you thought you could easily tell the tale, but now you are on your feet you find that it is not quite so easy to clothe in words the thoughts which floated through your brain.

What is beauty? Cold-blooded word-mongers answer *fitness*. And certainly there is fitness in all loveliness. But do not tell me that beauty is mere fitness, for I have seen a world of fitness in this world which, nevertheless, seemed to me to be inexpressibly ugly and unlovable. A wise man tells me that beauty is a *proportion*. But neither is this a full description by many a league. No doubt it is desirable that the features should be well balanced—the eyes should be fitly set, no one feature should be exaggerated and none should be dwarfed—

"In nature what affects our hearts,
Is not the exactness of peculiar parts:
'Tis not a lip nor eye we beauty call,
But the joint force and full result of all."

Harmony is beauty. Yet I have seen the chiseled marble fashioned with skillful art into a well-near perfect form which did not, could not, impress me with a sense of loveliness.

There stands in one of the halls of the Vatican a statue of Antinous. Every feature in that statue is perfect in itself and in complete harmony with all the rest. You could not find the slightest fault with eye or nose or mouth. It is, indeed, as much the ideal of male beauty as the Venus is of female charms, yet no one could ever have been enchanted with the statue, or have felt affection to the form which it represents. There is no expression whatever in the features! Everything is so adjusted and proportioned that you need a divergence to relieve you. The materialism is so carefully measured out that there needs a stir, a break in the harmony, to give it at least some semblance of a soul! Beauty, then, consists not in mere harmony, nor in balancing the features.

Loveliness surely is attractiveness. Yes, but that is another way of saying you do not know what it is. It is a something that attracts you and compels you to exclaim, "Nothing under Heaven does allure so strongly!" We feel its power; we become its slaves; but we cannot write with pen of cold steel, nor could we write even with a pen of lightning, a description of what it is. How, then, can I—enamored, entranced, enraptured as I am with Him whom my soul loves—how can I speak of Him? He is altogether lovely! Where shall I find words, terms, expressions that shall fitly set Him forth? Unless the Eternal Spirit shall raise me up out of myself, I must forever be incapable of setting forth the Well-Beloved!

Besides, were I baffled by nothing else, there is this— that the beauty of Christ is mysterious. It surpasses all the comeliness of human form. He may have had great beauty according to the flesh. That I cannot tell, but I should imagine that such a perfect soul as His must have inhabited a perfectly molded body. Never yet did you or I gaze with satisfaction upon the work of any painter who has tried to picture our Lord Jesus Christ. We have not blamed the great masters, but we have felt that the effort surpassed their powers. How could they photograph the sun? The loftiest conceptions of great artists, in this case, fall far short of the mark.

When the brightness of the Father's Glory is the subject the canvas glows in vain. Art sits at her easel and produces diligently many a draft of the sacred features, but they are all failures and they must be. Who shall ever depict Immanuel, God-With-Us? I suppose that, by-and-by, when our Lord had entered upon His active life and encountered its struggles, His youthful beauty was marred with lines of sadness and sorrow. Still His courage so overshadowed His cares—the mercy He showed so surpassed the misery He shared and the Grace He dispensed so exceeded the griefs that He carried, that a halo of real Glory must always have shone around His brow!

His Countenance must still have been lovely even when surrounded with the clouds of care and grief. How can we describe the marred visage? It is a great mystery, but a sure fact that in our Lord's marred Countenance His beauty is best seen. Anguish gave Him a loveliness which otherwise He had not reached. His passion put the finishing touches upon His unrivalled loveliness. But, Brothers and Sisters, I am not about to speak of Christ's loveliness after the *flesh*, for we now, after the flesh, know Him no more. It is His *moral* and *spiritual* beauty of which the spouse in the son most sweetly says, "Yes, He is altogether lovely." The loveliness which the eye dotes on is mere varnish when compared with that which dwells in virtue and holiness! The worm will devour the loveliness of skin and flesh, but a lovely character will endure forever.

I. THIS IS RARE PRAISE. Let that be our first head. This is rare praise. What if I say it is unique? For of no other being could it be said, "Yes, he is altogether lovely." It means, first, that all that is in Him is lovely, perfectly lovely. There is no point in our Lord Jesus that you could improve. To paint the rose were to spoil its ruddy hue.

To tint the lily, for He is lily as well as rose, were to mar its whiteness. Each virtue in our Lord is there in a state of absolute perfection—it could not be more fully developed. If you were able to conceive of each virtue at its ripest stage it would be found in Him. In the matter of transparent ingenuousness and sterling honesty, did ever man speak or act so truthfully as He?

Ask, on the other hand, for sympathizing tenderness and love—was ever any so gentle as Jesus? Do you want reverence to God? How He bows before the Father! Do you want boldness before men? How He beards the Pharisees! You could not better anything which you find in Jesus. Wherever you shall cast your eyes, they may rest with satisfaction, for the best of the best of the best is to be seen in Him! He is altogether lovely at every separate point, so that the spouse, when she began with His head, descended to His feet and then lifting her eyes upward, again, upon a return voyage of delight, she looked into His Countenance and summed up all that she had seen in one sentence, "He is altogether lovely." This is rare praise!

And He is all that is lovely. In each one of His people you will find something that is lovely—in one there is faith, in another abounding love—in one, tenderness, in another, courage. But you do not find *all* good things in any one saint—at least not all of them in full perfection. But you find all virtues in Jesus and each one of them at its best! If you would take the best quality of one saint and the best quality of another—yes, the best out of each and all the myriads of His people—you would find no Grace or goodness among them which Jesus does not possess in the fullest degree and in the highest perfection! He combines all the virtues and gives them sweetness over and beyond ourselves.

In flowers you have a separate beauty belonging to each. No one flower is just like another—each one blushes with its own loveliness. But in our Lord these separate and distinct beauties are found united in one. Christ is the flower in which all the beauties of the garden of perfection are bound up. Each gem has its own radiance—the diamond is not like the ruby, nor the ruby like the emerald—but Christ is that ring in which you have sapphire, ruby, diamond, emerald set in choice order, so that **each one heightens the other's brilliance.** Look not for anything lovely out of Jesus, for He has all the loveliness! All perfections are in Him making up one consummate perfection—and all the loveliness which is to be seen elsewhere is but a reflection of His own unrivalled charms.

In Jesus Christ—this, moreover, is rare praise again—there is nothing that is unlovely. You have a friend whom you greatly admire and fondly esteem, of whom, nevertheless, I doubt not you have often said to yourself in an undertone, "I wish I could take away a little of the rough edge of his manners here and there." You never thought that of Christ! You have observed of one man that he is so bold as to be sometimes rude and of another that he is so bland and amiable that he is apt to be effeminate. You have said, "That sweetness of his is exceedingly good, but I wish that it were qualified with sterner virtues." But there is *nothing* to tone down or alter in our Divine Lord. He is altogether lovely!

Have you not, sometimes, in describing a friend, been obliged to forget, or omit, some rather prominent characteristic when you wished to make a favorable impression? You have had to paint him as the artist once painted Oliver Cromwell—the great wart over the eyebrow was purposely left out of the portrait. Cromwell, you know, said "Paint me as I am, or not at all." We have, however, often felt that it was kind to leave out the warts when we were talking of those we esteemed and to whom we would pay a graceful tribute. But there is nothing to leave out in Christ, nothing to hold back, or to guard, or to extenuate! In Him is nothing redundant, nothing overgrown. He is altogether lovely.

You never need put the finger over the scar in His case, as Apelles did when he painted his hero. No, tell it all out—reveal the details of His private life and secret thoughts—they need no concealment! Lay bare the very heart of Christ, for that is the *essence* of love and loveliness! Speak of His death-wounds, for in His scars there is more beauty than in the uninjured comeliness of another. And even when He lies dead in the tomb He is more comely than the immortal angels of God at their best estate! Nothing about our Lord needs to be concealed! Even His Cross, at which His enemies stumble, is to be daily proclaimed and it will be seen to be one of His choicest beauties.

Frequently, too, in commending a friend whom you highly appreciated, you have been prone to ask for consideration of his position and to make excuse for blemishes which you would gladly persuade us are less actual than apparent. You have remarked how admirably he acts considering his surroundings. Conscious that someone would hint at an imperfection, you have anticipated the current of conversation by alluding to the circumstances which rendered it so difficult for your friend to act commendably. You have felt the need of showing that others influenced him, or that infirmity restrained him. Did you ever feel inclined to apologize for Christ? Did He not always stand unbending beneath life's pressure—upright and unmoved amidst the storms and tempests of an evil world?

The vilest calumnies have been uttered against Him in the age just past which produced creatures similar to Thomas Paine, but they never required an answer! And as for the more refined attacks of our modern skepticism, they are, for the most part, unworthy, even, of contempt! They fall beneath the glance of the Truth of God, withered by the glance of the eye of honesty. We never feel concerned to vindicate the Character of

Jesus—we know it to be safe against all comers. No man has been able to conjure up an accusation against Jesus. They seek false witnesses, but their testimony agrees not together. The sharp arrows of slander fall blunted from the shield of His perfectness. Oh, no—He is altogether lovely in this sense—that there is nothing whatever in Him that is not lovely! You may look and look and look again, but there is nothing in Him that will not bear scrutiny, world without end!

Taking the Lord Jesus Christ as a whole—this is what our text intends to tell us—He is inexpressibly lovely, altogether lovely! The words are packed as tightly as they can be, but the meaning is greater than the words. Some translate the passage, "He is all desires," and it is a good translation, too, and contains a grand truth. Christ is so lovely that all you can desire of loveliness is in Him and even if you were to sit down and task your imagination and burden your understanding to contrive, to invent, to fashion the ideal of something that should be inimitable—yes, (to utter a paradox)—if you could labor to conceive something which should be inconceivably lovely, yet you would not reach to the perfection of Christ Jesus!

He is above not only all we think, but all we dream. Do you believe this? Dear Hearers, do you think of Jesus in this fashion? We speak what we know and testify what we have seen. But no man among you will receive our witness until he can say, "I, also, have seen Him, and having seen Him, I set to my seal that He is altogether lovely."

II. And now, secondly, as this is rare praise, so likewise IT IS PERPETUAL PRAISE. You may say of Christ whenever you look at Him, "Yes, He is altogether lovely." He always was so. As God over all, He is blessed forever, Amen. When, in addition to His Godhead, He assumed our mortal clay, was He not inimitably lovely then? The Baby in Bethlehem was the most beautiful sight that ever the world beheld. No fairer flower ever bloomed in the garden of creation than the mind of that Youth of Nazareth gradually unfolding, as He "grew, and waxed strong in spirit, filled with wisdom: and the Grace of God was upon Him."

All the while He lived on earth, what moral perfections, what noble qualities, what spiritual charms were about His sacred Person! His life among men is a succession of charming pictures and He was lovely in His bitter passion, when as the thick darkness overshadowed His soul He prayed, in an agony of desire, "Not My will, but Yours, be done." **The bloody sweat did not disfigure Him, but rather adorned Him!** And oh, was He not lovely when He died? Without resentment He interceded for His murderers. His patience, His self-possession, His piety as "the faithful Martyr," have fixed as the meridian of time the hour when He said, "It is finished," and "bowed His head," and "cried with a loud voice, Father, into Your hands I commend My spirit."

He is lovely in His Resurrection from the dead—beyond description lovely! Not a word of accusation did He utter against His cruel persecutors, though He had risen clothed with all power in Heaven and in earth! With such tender sympathy did He make Himself known to His sorrowing disciples that, despite the waywardness of their unbelief, their hearts' instinct told them it was "the same Jesus." He is altogether lovely. He will be lovely when He comes with solemn pomp and sound of trumpet—with escort of mighty angels—and brings all His saints who have departed with Him and calls up those that are alive and remain on the earth till His advent, to meet Him in the air.

Oh, how lovely He will appear to the two throngs who will presently join in one company! How admirable will His appearance be! How eyes, ears, hearts and voices will greet Him! With what unanimity the host redeemed by blood will account their highest acclamations as a trivial tribute to His honor and glory! "He is altogether lovely." Yes, and He shall be lovely forever and ever when your eyes and mine shall eternally find their Heaven in beholding Him. "Jesus Christ, the same yesterday, today, and forever," is always worthy of this word of praise—"altogether lovely." Let us retrace our steps for a minute. The more we study the four Gospels, the more charmed we are with the Gospel—for as a modern author has well said—"The Gospels, like the Gospel, are most Divine because they are most human."

As followers of Jesus, rank yourselves with those men who companied with Him all the time that He went in and out among them and you shall find Him lovely in all conditions. Lovely when He talks to a leper and touches and heals him; lovely by the bedside when He takes the fever-stricken patient by the hand and heals her; lovely by the wayside, when He greets the blind beggar, puts His finger on his eyes and bids him see. He is lovely when He stands on the sinking vessel and rebukes the waves; lovely when He meets the bier and rekindles the life that had expired; lovely when He visits the mourners, goes with the sisters of Bethany to the newly-made grave and weeps, and groans, and—majestically lovely—bids the dead come forth!

Lovely is He when He rides through the streets of Jerusalem upon a colt, the foal of an ass. Oh, had we been there, we would have plucked the palm branches and we would have taken off our garments to strew the way! Hosanna, lovely Prince of Peace! But He was just as lovely when He came from the garden with His face all smeared with bloody sweat. He was just as lovely when they said, "Crucify Him, Crucify Him!" He was just as lovely and, if possible, more so, when down those sacred cheeks there dripped the cursed spit from the rough soldiers' mouths—yes, and loveliest, to my eyes, loveliest of all, when mangled, wounded, fainting, bruised, dying, He said, "My God, My God, why have You forsaken Me?" uttering a plaintive cry of utmost grief from the felon's gallows where He died. Yes, view Him where you will, in any place, is He not—I speak to you who know Him, and not to those who never saw Him with the eyes of faith—is He not, in the night and in the day, on the sea and on the land, on earth and in Heaven, altogether lovely?

He is lovely in all His offices! What an entrancing sight to see the King in His beauty, with His diadem upon His head as He now sits in yonder world of brightness! How charming to view Him as a Priest, with the Urim and Thummim, wearing the names of His people bejeweled on His breastplate! And what a vision of simple beauty to see Him as a Prophet teaching His people in touching parables of homely interest, of whom they said, "Never man spoke like this Man!" The very tones of His voice and the glance of His eyes made His eloquence so supreme that it enthralled men's hearts! Yes, He is lovely, altogether lovely in any and every Character. We know not which best befits Him, the highest or the lowest positions. Let Him be what He may—Lamb or Shepherd, Brother or Kin, Savior or Master, Foot-Washer or Lord—in every relation He is altogether lovely!

Get a view of Him, my Brothers and Sisters, from any point and see whether He is not lovely. Do you remember the first sight you ever had of Him? It was on a day when your eyes were red with weeping over sin and you expected to see the Lord dressed in anger coming forth to destroy you! Oh, it was the happiest sight I ever saw when I beheld my sins rolling into His sepulcher and, when looking up, I beheld Him, my Substitute, bleeding on the tree! Altogether lovely was He that day! Since then, Providence has given us a varied experience and taken us to different points of view that we might look at Christ and see Him under many aspects. We look at statues from several standpoints if we would criticize them. A great many in London are hideous from all points of view—others are very well if you look at them this way, but if you go over yonder and look from another point the artist appears to have utterly failed.

Now, Beloved, look at Jesus from any point you like and He is at His best from each and every corner! You have been in prosperity—God multiplied your children and blessed your basket and your store—was Jesus lovely then? Assuredly He was the light of your delights! Nothing He had given you vied with Himself. He rose in your hearts superior to His own best gifts. But you tell me that you have been very sick and you have lost one after another of your dear ones. Your means have been reduced; you have come down in the world—say, then, is Jesus lovely now? I know that you will reply, "Yes, more than ever is Christ delightful in my eyes." Well, you have had very happy times and you have been on the mount of hallowed friendship. The other Sunday morning many of us were up there and thought, like Peter, that we should like to stay there forever—and is not Jesus lovely when He is transfigured and we are with Him?

Yes, but at another time you are down in the depths with Jonah, at the bottom of the sea. Is not Christ lovely then, too? Yes, even there He hears our prayers out of His holy temple and brings us up from the deep abyss! We shall soon lie dying. Oh, my Brothers and Sisters, what brave talk God's people have often given us about their Lord when they have been on the edge of the grave! That seems to be a time when the Well-Beloved takes the veil off His face altogether and sits by the bedside and lets His children look into His face and see Him as He is. I guarantee you the saints forget the ghastliness of death when their hearts are ravished with the loveliness of Christ!

Yes, up to this point Jesus has been lovely. And now, let us add that He will always be so. You know there are persons whom you account beautiful when you are young, but when you grow older in years, riper in judgment and more refined in taste, you meet with others who look far more beautiful. Now, what do you think of your Lord? Have you met with anyone, in fact or in fable, more beautiful than He? You thought Him charming when you were but a baby in Grace. What do you think of Him now? Taste, you know, grows and develops with education—an article of art which fascinated you years ago has no longer any charms for you because your taste is raised. Has your spiritual taste outgrown your Lord's beauties?

Come, Brothers and Sisters, does Christ go *down* as you learn the Truth of God more exactly and acquaint yourself more fully with Him? Oh no! You prize Him a thousand times more today than you did when the first impression of His goodness was formed in your mind! Some things which look very lovely at a distance lose their loveliness when you get near to them—but is it not true, (I am sure it is), that the nearer you get to Christ the lovelier He is? Some things are only beautiful in your eyes for their novelty—you admire them when you have seen them once—if you were to see them a dozen times you would not care much about them. What do you say about my Master? Is it not true that the more you see Him, the more you know Him and the more familiar your communion with Him, the more He rises in your esteem? I know it is so and well, therefore, did the spouse say, "He is altogether lovely."

Christ is altogether lovely in this respect—that when men reproach Him and rail at Him, He is often all the lovelier in His people's eyes. I guarantee you Christ has been better known by the Burnside in Scotland by His covenanting people than ever He has been seen under the roof of cathedral architecture! Away there in lonely glens, amid the mosses and hills, where Covenanters met for fear of Claverhouse and his dragoons, the Lord Jesus has shone forth like the sun in his strength! We have, nowadays, to be satisfied with His moonlight face, but in persecuting days His children have seen His sun face, and oh, how glad they have been! Hear how the saints sing in prison! Listen to their charming notes, even on the rack, when the glory of His Presence fills their souls with Heaven on earth and makes them defy the torments of the flesh!

The Lord Jesus is more lovely to the soul that can bear reproach for Him than He is to any other. Put the Cross on His back if you will, but we love Him all the better for that! Nail up His hands, but we love Him all the better for that! Now fasten His feet, yes, but our soul melts with love to Him and she feels new reasons for loving Him when she beholds the nails! Now stand around the Cross, you worldlings, and mock Him if you will. Taunt and jest, jeer and jibe—these do but make us love better the great and glorious One who "made Himself of no reputation and took upon Him the form of a Servant, and being found in fashion as a Man, humbled Himself and became obedient unto death, even the death of the Cross."

Beloved, you shall keep on looking at Christ from all these points of view till you get to Heaven and each time you shall be more enamored of Him! When you reach the celestial City and see Him face to face then shall you say, "The half has not been told us," but even here below Christ is altogether lovely to His people.

III. I leave that head just to notice, in the third place, that though this praise is rare praise and perpetual praise, yet IT IS ALSO TOTALLY INSUFFICIENT PRAISE. Do you say that He is altogether lovely? It is not enough! It is not a thousandth part enough! No tongue of man or tongue of angel can ever set forth His unutterable beauties! "Oh," you say, "but it is a great word, though short—very full of meaning though soon spoken— 'altogether lovely.'" I tell you it is a poor word. It is a word of despair! It is a word which the spouse uttered because she had been trying to describe her Lord and she could not do it—and so she put this down in very desperation, as much as to say—"There, the task is too great for me. I will end it. This is all I can say. 'Yes, He is altogether lovely.'"

I am sure John Berridge was right when he said—
> *"Living tongues are dumb at best,*
> *We must die to speak of Christ."*

Brothers and Sisters, the praise of the text is insufficient praise, I know, because it is praise given by one who had never seen Him in His glory. It is *Old Testament* praise, this, that He is altogether lovely—praise uttered upon *report* rather than upon actual view of Him. Truly, I know not how to say it better, but I shall know one day! Till then I will speak His praise as best I can, though it falls far short of His infinite excellence. Our text is cloth of gold, but it is not fit for our Beloved to put the sole of His feet upon. He deserves better than this, for this is only the praise of a Church that had not seen Him die and had not seen Him rise—and had not seen Him in splendor at the Divine right hand!

"Well," you say, "try if you can, to do better." No, I will not, because if I did praise Him better, the style would not last long, for He is coming quickly and the best thing the best speaker could ever say of Him will be put out of date by the majesty of His appearing! His chariot is waiting at His door right now and He may soon come forth from His secret chambers and be among us and oh, the Glory—oh the Glory! Paul, you know, stole a glance through the lattices one day when he was caught up into the third Heaven. Somebody said to me, "I wonder why Paul did not tell us what he saw?" Yes, but what he saw he might not tell and the words he heard were words which it were not lawful for a man to utter and yet live among this evil generation. We shall hear those words, ourselves, soon, and see those sights not many days hence, so let it stand as it does, "He is altogether lovely."

But when you have thus summed up all that our poor tongues can express, you must not say, "Now we have described Him." Oh no, Sirs, you have but held a candle to this glorious sun—He is such an One as thoughts cannot compass, much less, language describe! I leave this point with the reflection that God intends to describe Him and set Him forth one day. He is waiting patiently, for longsuffering is part of Christ's Character and God is setting forth the longsuffering of Christ in the patient waiting of these 1,800 years. But the day shall presently dawn and usher in the everlasting age when Christ shall be better seen; for every eye shall see Him and every tongue confess that He is Lord! The whole earth will, one day, be sweet with the praise of Jesus!

Earth, did I say? This alabaster box of Christ's sweetness has too much fragrance in it for the world to keep it all to itself! The sweetness of our Lord's Person will rise above the stars and perfume worlds unknown! It will fill Heaven itself! Eternity shall be occupied with declaring the praises of Jesus! Seraphs shall sing of it; angels shall harp it; the redeemed shall declare it! He is altogether lovely! The cycles of eternity, as they revolve, shall only confirm the statement of the blood-redeemed that He is altogether lovely! O that the days were come when we shall bow with them and sing with them! Wait a little while and be not weary and you shall be Home—and then you shall know that I spoke the truth when I said that this was insufficient praise! Earth is too narrow to contain Him! Heaven is too little to hold Him! Eternity, itself, too short for the utterance of all His praises!

IV. So I close with this last thought, which may God bless for practical uses. This praise is VERY SUGGESTIVE. If Christ is altogether lovely it suggests a question. Suppose I never saw His loveliness? Suppose that in this house there should be souls that never saw anything in Christ to make them love Him? If you were to go to some remote island where beauty consisted in having one eye, a twisted mouth and a sea-green complexion, you would say, "Those people are strange beings." Such are the people of this world! *Spiritual* beauty is not appreciated by them! This world appreciates the man who makes money, however reckless he may be of the welfare of others while scheming to heap up riches for himself.

As for the man who slays his fellow creatures by thousands, they mount him on a bronze horse, put him on an arch, or they pile up a column and set him as near Heaven as they can. He slew his thousands! He died blood-red—he was an emperor, a tyrant, a conqueror—the world feels his power and pays its homage! As for this Jesus, He only gave His life for men. He was only pure and perfect, the mirror of disinterested love. The vain world cannot see in Him a virtue to admire. It is a blind world, a fool world, a world that lies in the Wicked One! Not to discern the beauties of Jesus is an evidence of terrible depravity!

Have you, my dear Friend, to frankly confess that you were never enamored of Him who was holy, harmless and undefiled and went about doing good? Then let this come home to you—the question is not as to whether Christ is lovely or not, the mistake is here—you have not a spiritually enlightened eye, a fine moral perception, nor even a well-regulated conscience, or you would see His loveliness at once. You are evil and blind! God help you to feel this! Do you not love Christ? Then let me ask you *why* you do not? There was never a man that could give a reason for not loving Him, neither is there such a reason to be discovered! He is altogether lovely! In nothing is He unlovable.

Oh I wish that the good Spirit of God would whisper in your heart and incline you to say, "I will see about this Christ. I will read of Him. I will look at the four portraits of Him painted by the Evangelists and if He is, indeed, thus lovely, no doubt He will win my heart as He appears to have won the hearts of others." I pray He may. But do not, I pray you, continue to deny Christ your love. It is all you can give Him. It is a poor thing, but He values it. He would sooner have your heart than all the gold in Europe. He would sooner have the heart of a poor servant girl or of a poor humble laborer upon the soil than the Queen's diadem. He loves love! Love is His gem—His jewel. He delights to win it and if He is, indeed, altogether lovely, let Him have it!

You have known people, I dare say, whom you could not help loving. They never had to say to you "Love me," for you were captivated at once by the very sight of them. In like manner many have only received one beam of light from the Holy Spirit and have thereby seen who Jesus was and they have at once said of Him, "You have ravished my heart with one look of Your eyes" and so it has been that all of their life they have loved their Lord. Now, the praise is suggestive still further. "Is Christ altogether lovely? Then do I love Him? As a child of God, do I love Him as much as I ought? I do love Him. Yes, blessed be His name, I do love Him. But what a poor, cold, chill love it is. How few are the sacrifices I make for Him. How few are the offerings that I present to Him. How little is the fellowship that I maintain with Him."

Brother, Sister, is there a rival in your heart? Do you allow anyone to come in between you and the "Altogether Lovely"? If so, chase the intruder out! Christ must have all your heart and let me tell you, the more we love Him, the more bliss we shall have. A soul that is altogether given up to the love of Christ lives above care and sorrow. It has care and sorrow, but the love of Christ kills all the bitterness by its inexpressible sweetness! I cannot tell you how near a man may live to Heaven, but I am persuaded that a very large proportion of the bliss of Heaven may be enjoyed before we go there. There is one conduit pipe through which heavenly joy will flow and if you draw from it, you may have as much as you will.

"Abide in Me" says Christ. And if you abide in His love you shall have His joy fulfilled in yourselves so that your joy may be full. You will have more capacious vessels in Heaven, but even now the little vessel that you have can be filled up to the brim by knowing the inexpressible loveliness of Jesus and surrendering your hearts to it! Oh that I could rise to something better than myself! I often feel like a chick in the egg—I am pecking my way out and I cannot get clear of my prison. Gladly would I chip the shell, come forth to freedom, develop wings and soar heavenward, singing on the way! Would God that were our portion! If anything can help us get out of the shell and to begin to rise and sing, it must be a full and clear perception that Jesus is altogether lovely!

Come; let us be married to Him afresh tonight. Come, believing hearts, yield again to His charms! Surrender yourselves, again, to the supremacy of His affection. Let us have the love of our espousals renewed. As you come to His table, think of the lips of Christ, of which the spouse had been speaking before she uttered my text—"His mouth is most sweet." There are three things about Christ's mouth that are very sweet. The first is His Word—you have *heard* that. The second is His breath. Come, Holy Spirit, make Your people *feel* that. And the third is His *kiss*. May every believing soul have that sweet token of His eternal love!

Forgive my ramblings. May God bless to all His people the word that has been spoken. May some that never knew my Master ask to know Him tonight. Go home and seek Him. Read the Word to find Him. Cry to Him in prayer and He will be found of you. He is so lovely that I should not live without loving Him and I shall deeply regret it if any one of you shall spend another 24 hours without having had a sight of His Divine face by faith.

THE ROSE AND THE LILY

DELIVERED ON LORD'S-DAY MORNING,
DECEMBER 8, 1867,
BY C. H. SPURGEON,

AT THE METROPOLITAN TABERNACLE,
NEWINGTON.

*"I am the rose of Sharon,
and the lily of the valleys."*

Song of Solomon 2:1

HERE are sweet flowers blooming serenely in this wintry weather. In the garden of the soul you may gather fragrant flowers at all seasons of the year. And although the soul's garden, like every other, has its winter, yet, strange to say, no sooner do the roses and the lilies mentioned in the text begin to bloom than the winter flies and the summer smiles! Outside, in your garden, the summer brings the roses, but within the enclosure of the *heart* the roses and lilies create the summer.

I trust that we, this morning, may have Divine Grace to walk abroad in the fields of heavenly contemplation to admire the matchless charms of Him whose cheeks are as a bed of spices, as sweet flowers—whose lips are like lilies dropping sweet smelling myrrh. May our hearts interpret the language of our text and sing—

"Is He a rose?
Not Sharon yields
Such fragrance in all her fields:
Or, if the lily He assumes,
The valleys bless the rich perfume."

It is our Lord who speaks: "I am the rose of Sharon." How is it that He utters His own commendation, for it is an old and true adage, that "self-praise is no recommendation"? None but vain creatures ever praise themselves, and yet Jesus often praises Himself! He says, "I am the good Shepherd." "I am the Bread of Life." "I am meek and lowly of heart." And in many speeches He is frequently declaring His own excellencies, yet Jesus is not vain! Scorned be the thought!

I said if any creature praised itself it must be vain, and that, too, is true. How then shall we solve the riddle? Is not this the answer, that He is no *creature* at all, and therefore comes not beneath the rule? For the creature to praise itself is vanity, but for the Creator to praise Himself—for the Lord God to manifest and show forth His own glory is becoming and proper. Hear how He extols His own wisdom and power in the end of the book of Job and see if it is not most seemly as the Lord Himself proclaims it!

Is not God constantly ruling both Providence and Grace for the manifestation of His own glory, and do we not all freely consent that no motive short of this would be worthy of the Divine mind? So, then, because Christ talks thus of Himself, since no man dare call Him vainglorious, I gather an indirect proof of His Deity and bow down before Him! And I bless Him that He gives me this incidental evidence of His being no creature, but the Uncreated One Himself. An old Scotch woman once said, "He is never so bonnie as when He is commending Himself." And we all feel it so—no words appear more suitable out of His own lips than these, "I am the rose of Sharon, and the lily of the valleys."

Our Lord, when He thus praises Himself, doubtless does so for an excellent reason, namely, that no one can possibly reveal Him to the sons of men but Himself. No lips can tell the love of Christ to the heart till Jesus Himself shall speak within. Descriptions all fall flat and tame unless the Holy Spirit fills them with life and power—till our Immanuel reveals Himself within the recesses of the heart the soul sees Him not. If you would see the sun, would you light your candles? Would you gather together the common means of illumination and seek, in that way, to behold the orb of day?

No, the wise man knows that the sun must reveal itself and only by its own blaze can that mighty lamp be seen. It is so with Christ. Unless He so manifest Himself to us as He does *not* unto the world, we cannot behold Him. He must say to *us*, "I am the rose of Sharon," or else all the declarations of man that He is the rose of Sharon will fall short of the mark. "Blessed are you, Simon Barjona," said He to Peter, "for flesh and blood have not revealed this unto you." Purify flesh and blood by any educational process you may select. Elevate mental faculties to the highest degree of intellectual power, yet none of these can reveal Christ! The Spirit of God must come with power and overshadow the man with His wings—and then in that mystic Holy of Holies the Lord Jesus must display Himself to the sanctified eye as He does not unto the purblind sons of men.

Christ must be His own mirror. As the diamond alone can cut the diamond, so He alone can display Himself. Is it not clear enough to us all that Jesus, being God, befittingly praises Himself? And we, being frail creatures, He must necessarily commend Himself or we should never be able to perceive His beauty at all! Each reason is sufficient. Both are overwhelming. It is most suitable that Jesus should preach Jesus, that Love should teach us love. Beloved, happy are those men to whom our Lord familiarly unveils His beauties! He is the rose, but it is not given unto all men to perceive His fragrance. He is the fairest of lilies, but few are the eyes which have gazed upon His matchless purity.

He stands before the world without form or comeliness—a root out of a dry ground—rejected by the vain, and despised by the proud. The great mass of this bleary-eyed world can see nothing of the ineffable glories of Immanuel. Only where the Spirit has touched the eyes with eye salve, quickened the heart with Divine life, and educated the soul to a heavenly taste—only there is that love word of my text heard and understood, "I am the rose of Sharon, and the lily of the valleys." "To you that believe He is precious." To you He is the cornerstone. To you He is the rock of your salvation, your All in All. But to others He is "a stone of stumbling and a rock of offense, even to them which stumble at the Word, being disobedient."

Let it be our prayer, before we advance a single foot further, that our Redeemer would now reveal Himself to His own chosen people and favor each one of us with at least a glimpse of His all-conquering charms! May the King Himself draw near unto His guests this morning, and as of old, when it was winter He walked in the temple of Solomon's porch, so may He walk in the midst of this waiting assembly.

I. First, this morning, I shall speak with you a little, as I may be helped by the Holy Spirit, upon THE MOTIVES OF OUR LORD IN THUS COMMENDING HIMSELF. I take it that He has designs of love in this speech. He would have all His people rich in high and happy thoughts concerning His blessed Person. Jesus is not content that His brethren should think meanly of Him. It is His pleasure that His espoused ones should be delighted with His beauty, and that He should be King and Lord of their spirits. He would have us possess an adoring admiration for Him joined with most cheerful and happy thoughts towards Him.

We are not to count Him as a bare necessity, like bread and water, but we are to regard Him as a luxurious delicacy, as a rare and ravishing delight, comparable to the rose and the lily. Our Lord, you observe, expresses Himself here poetically, "I am the rose of Sharon." Dr. Watts, when he had written his delightful hymns, was the subject of Dr. Johnson's criticism. And that excellent lexicographer, who wrote with great authority upon all literary matters, entirely missed his mark when he said that the themes of religion were so few and so prosaic that they were not adapted for the poet—they were not such as could allow of the flight of wing which poetry required. Alas, Dr. Johnson! How little could you have entered into the spirit of these things, for if there is any place where poetry may indulge itself to the uttermost, it is in the realm of the Infinite!

Jordan's streams are as pure as Helicon, and Siloam's brook as inspiring as the Castilian fount! Heathen Parnassus has not half the elevation of the Christian's Tabor, let critics judge as they may! This book of Solomon's Song is poetry of the very highest kind to the *spiritual* mind, and throughout Scripture the sublime and beautiful are as much at home as the degree of poetical faculty is consecrated to Him, and that lofty thoughts and soaring conceptions concerning Himself are no intruders, but are bound to pay homage at His Cross! Jesus would have us enjoy the highest thoughts of

Him that the most sublime prose can possibly convey to us! And His motives I shall labor to lay before you.

Doubtless, He commends Himself because high thoughts of Christ will enable us to act consistently with our relations towards Him. The saved soul is espoused to Christ. Now, in the marriage estate it is a great assistance to happiness if the wife has high ideas of her husband. In the marriage union between the soul and Christ, this is exceedingly necessary. Listen to the words of the Psalm, "He is your Lord; and worship you Him." Jesus is our Husband, and is no more to be named Baal, that is your master. He is to be Ishi, your Man, your Husband. Yet at the same time He is our Lord, "For the husband is the head of the wife, even as Christ is the Head of the Church: and He is the Savior of the body."

When the wife despises her husband and looks down upon him, the order of nature is broken and the household is out of joint. And if our soul should ever come to despise Christ, it can no longer stand in its true relation to Him. But the more loftily we see Christ enthroned, and the more lowly we are when bowing before the foot of the Throne, the more truly shall we be prepared to act our part in the economy of Grace towards our Lord Jesus. Brothers and Sisters, your Lord Christ desires you to think well of Him that you may submit cheerfully to His authority and so be a better spouse to this best of Husbands.

Moreover, our Master knows that high thoughts of Him increase our love. Men will not readily love that which they do not highly esteem. Love and esteem go together. There is a love of pity but that would be far out of place in reference to our exalted Head. If we are to love Him at all it must be with the love of admiration—and the higher that admiration shall rise, the more vehemently will our love flame forth. My Brothers and Sisters in Christ, I beseech you think much of your Master's excellencies. Study Him in His primeval Glory, before He took upon Himself your nature! Think of the mighty love which drew Him from His starry throne to die upon the cross of shame! Consider well the omnipotent affection which made Him stretch His hands to the nails and yield His heart to the spear! Admire Him as you see Him conquering, in His weakness, over all the powers of Hell, and by His suffering overthrowing all the hosts of your sins so that they cannot rise against you any more forever!

See Him now risen, no more to die! Crowned, no more to be dishonored! Glorified, no more to suffer! Bow before Him, hail Him in the halls of your inner nature as the Wonderful, the Counselor, the Mighty God within your spirits, for only thus will your love to Him be what it should. A high esteem of Christ, moreover, as He well knows, is very necessary to our comfort. Beloved, when you esteem Christ very highly, the things of this world become of small account with you and their loss is not so heavily felt. If you feel your losses and crosses to be such ponderous weights that the wings of Christ's love cannot lift you up from the dust, surely you have made too much of the world and too little of Him!

I see a pair of balances. I see in this one the death of a child, or the loss of a beloved relative. But I perceive in the other scale the great love of Christ! Now we shall see which will weigh the more with the man—if Jesus throws the light affliction up aloft, it is well—but if the trouble outweighs Jesus, then it is ill with us, indeed. If you are so depressed by your trials that you can by no means rejoice knowing your name is written in Heaven, then I think you do not love Jesus as you should. Get but delightful thoughts of Him and you will feel like a man who has lost a pebble but has preserved his diamond— like the man who has seen a few cast clouts and rotten rags consumed in the flames, but has saved his children from the conflagration. You will rejoice in your deepest distress because Christ is yours if you have a high sense of the preciousness of your Master!

Talk not of plasters that will draw out all pain from a wound! Speak not of medicines which will extirpate disease! The sweet love of Christ once clapped on to the deepest wound which the soul can ever know would heal it at once! A drop of the precious medicine of Jesus' love tasted in the soul would chase away all heart pains forever. Jesus, Jesus, Jesus, be within us and we make no choice of situations! Put us in Nebuchadnezzar's furnace—if You will walk the glowing coals as our Companion, we will fear no evil!

Further, our Lord would have us entertain great thoughts of Himself because this will quicken all the powers of our soul. I spoke to you just now of love receiving force from an esteem of Jesus. I might say the same of faith, or patience, or humility. Wherever Christ is highly esteemed all the faculties of the spiritual man exercise themselves with energy. I will judge your piety by this barometer—does Christ stand high or low with you? If you have thought little of Christ, if you have been content to live without His Presence—if you have cared little for His honor or if you have been neglectful of His Laws—then I know that your soul is sick! God grant that it may not be sick unto death!

But if the first thought of your spirit has been, "How can I honor Jesus?" If the daily desire of your soul has been, "O that I knew where I might find Him!" I tell you that you may have a thousand infirmities and may even scarcely know whether you are a child of God at all, and yet I am persuaded, beyond a doubt, that you are safe since Jesus is great in your esteem. I care not for your rags, what do you think of His royal apparel? I care not for your wounds, though they bleed in torrents—what do you think of *His* wounds? Are they like glittering rubies in your esteem? I think nothing the less of you, though you lie like Lazarus on the dunghill, and the dogs lick you! I judge you not by your poverty—what do you think of the King in His beauty?

Has He a glorious high throne in your heart? Would you set Him higher if you could? Would you be willing to die if you could but add another trumpet to the strain which proclaims His praise? Ah, then, it is well with you. Whatever you may think of yourself, if Christ is great to you, you shall be with Him before long. High thoughts of Jesus will set us upon high attempts for His honor. What will men not do when they are possessed with the passion of love? When once some master thought gets hold of the mind, others who have never felt the power of it think the man to be insane! They laugh at him and ridicule him. When the grand thought of love to God has gained full possession of the soul, men have been able to actually accomplish what other men have not even thought of doing. Love has laughed at impossibilities and proved that she is not to be quenched by many waters, nor drowned by floods.

Impassable woods have been made a footway for the Christian missionary. Through the dense jungle, steaming with malaria, men have passed bearing the message of the Truth of God; into the midst of hostile and savage tribes, weak and trembling *women*, even, have forced their way to tell of Jesus. No sea has been so stormy; no mountains have been so elevated that they could shut out the earnest spirit. No long nights of winter in Labrador or in Iceland have been able to freeze up the love of Christ in the Moravian's heart—it has not been possible for the zeal of the heir of Heaven to be overcome, though all the elements have combined with the cruelty of wicked men and with the malice of Hell itself.

Christ's people have been more than conquerors through Him that has loved them when His love has been shed abroad in their hearts by the Holy Spirit and they have had elevated thoughts of their Lord. I wish it were in my power to put this matter more forcibly, but I am persuaded, Brethren, that our Lord, in commending Himself to us this morning in the words of our text, does so with this as His motive—that by the power of His Spirit we may be led to esteem Him very highly in the inmost secret of our heart. And shall He speak to us in vain? Shall He stand in this pulpit, this morning, as He does in Spirit, and shall He say, "I am the rose of Sharon"? And shall we reply, "But we see not Your beauty"? Shall He add a double commendation, "I am the lily of the valley"? And shall our cold hearts reply, "But we admire not Your spotless purity"?

I trust we are not so utterly abandoned to spiritual blindness and ingratitude! Far rather, although we confess before Him that we do not admire Him as we should, we will add humbly, and with the tear of repentance in our eyes—

"Yes we love You and adore—
O for Grace to love You more."

II. Whatever may be the commendable motive for any
statement, yet it must not be made if it is not accurate,
and therefore, in the second place, I come to observe
OUR LORD'S JUSTIFICATION FOR THIS COMMENDATION,
which is abundantly satisfactory to all who know Him.
What our Lord says of Himself is strictly true. It falls
short of the mark, it is no exaggeration. Observe each
one of the words. He begins, "I am." Those two little
words I would not insist upon, but it is no straining of
language to say that even here we have a great deep.
What creature can, with exact truthfulness, say, "I am"?

As for man, whose breath is in his nostrils, he may rather
say, "I am not," than "I am." We are so short a time
here, and so quickly gone, that the ephemera which is
born and dies under the light of one day's sun is our
brother. Poor short-lived creatures, we change with
every moon and are inconsistent as the wave, frail as the
dust, feeble as a worm and fickle as the wind. Jesus says,
"I Am," and, blessed be His name, He can fairly claim the
attributes of self-existence and immutability. He said, "I
Am," in the days of His flesh. He says, "I Am," at this
hour—whatever He was He is! Whatever He has been to
any of His saints at any time, He is to us this day.

Come, my soul, rejoice in your unchangeable Christ, and
if you get no further than the first two words of the text,

you have a meal to stay your hunger, like Elijah's cakes in the strength of which he went for forty days. "I Am" in human flesh has become your Savior and your Lord!

"I am the rose." We understand from this that Christ is lovely. He selects one of the most charming of flowers to set forth Himself. All the beauties of all the creatures are to be found in Christ in greater perfection than in the creatures themselves—

> *"White and ruddy is my Beloved,*
> *All His heavenly beauties shine.*
> *Nature can't produce an object,*
> *Nor so glorious, so Divine.*
> *He has wholly*
> *Won my soul to realms above."*

"Whatever things are true, whatever things are honest, whatever things are just, whatever things are pure, whatever things are lovely, whatever things are of good report," all are to be found stored up in our Well-Beloved. Whatever there may be of beauty in the material world, Jesus Christ possesses all that in the spiritual world, only in a tenfold multiplication He is infinitely more beautiful in the garden of the soul and in the Paradise of God than the rose can be in the gardens of earth, though it is the universally acknowledged queen of flowers.

But the Spouse adds, "I am the rose of Sharon." This was the best and rarest of roses. Jesus is not "the rose" alone, but "the rose of Sharon," just as He calls His righteousness, "gold," and then adds, "the gold of Ophir"—the best of the best! Jesus, then is not only positively lovely, but superlatively the loveliest—

"None among the sons of men,
None among the heavenly train,
Can with Sharon's rose compare.
None so sweet and none so fair."

The Son of David takes the first place as the fairest among ten thousand. He is the sun, and all others are the stars. In His Presence all the feebler lights are hidden, for they are nothing and He is All in All. Blush for your deformities, you beauties of earth, when His perfections eclipse you! Away, you pageants, and you pompous triumphs of men! The King in His beauty transcends you all! Black are the heavens and dark is the day in comparison with Him!

Oh, to see Him face to face! This would be a vision for which life would be a glad exchange! For a vision of His face we could gladly be blind forever to all joys beside. Our Lord adds, "I am the lily," thus giving Himself a double commendation. Indeed, Jesus Christ deserves not to be praised doubly, but sevenfold. Yes, and unto seven times seven! Heap up all the metaphors that express loveliness. Bring together all the adjectives which describe delight and all human speech and all earth-born things shall fail to tell of Him. The rose with all its redness is not complete till the lily adds its purity and the two together are but dim reflections of our glorious Lord!

I learn from the text that in Christ Jesus you have a combination of contrasted excellencies. If He is red with the flush of courageous zeal, or red with triumph as He returns from Edom, He is the rose. But He is a warrior without sinful anger or cruel vengeance—He is as pure and spotless as the timid virgin who toys with the dove—He is therefore our snow-white lily. I see Him red as the rose in His sacrifice, as—

> *"From His head, His hands, His feet,*
> *Sorrow and love flow mingled down,"*

but I see Him white as the lily as He ascends on high in His perfect righteousness clothed in His white robe of victory to receive gifts for men. Our Beloved is a mingling of all perfections to make up one Perfection, and of all manner of sweetness to compose one complete Sweetness. Earth's choicest charms comingled feebly picture His abounding preciousness. He is the "lily of the valleys."

Does He intend, by that, to hint to us that He is a lily in His lowest estate, a lily of the valley? The carpenter's Son, living in poverty, wearing the common garb of the poor—is He the lily of the valleys? Yes, He is a lily to you and to me, poor dwellers in the lowlands. Up yonder He is a lily on the hilltops where all celestial eyes admire

Him. Down here, in these valleys of fears and cares, He is a lily, still, as fair as in Heaven. Our eyes can see His beauty, can see His beauty *now*, a lily to us this very day! Though we have not seen the King in His beauty, yet I say unto you that Solomon in all his glory was not arrayed like Jesus Christ in our eyes—as we see Him by faith in a glass darkly.

The words, having been opened up one by one, teach us that Christ is lovely to all our spiritual senses. The rose is delightful to the eyes, but it is also refreshing to the nostril, and the lily the same. So is Jesus. All the senses of the soul are ravished and satisfied with Him, whether it is the taste or feeling, the hearing, the sight, or the spiritual smell—all charms are in Jesus. Often when we have not seen the Anointed, we have perceived His Presence. Traveling on the Lake Lugano one morning, we heard the swell of the song of the nightingale, and the oars were stilled on the blue lake as we listened to the silver sounds. We could not see a single bird, nor do I know that we wished to—we were so content with the sweetness of the music.

Even so it is with our Lord. We may enter a house where He is loved and we may hear nothing concerning Christ and yet we may perceive clearly enough that He is there. A holy influence streams through the actions of the household, so that if Jesus is unseen, it is clear that He is not unknown. Go anywhere Jesus is, and though you do not actually hear His name, yet the sweet influence which flows from His love will be plainly enough discernible. Our Lord is so lovely that even the recollection of His love is sweet. Take the rose of Sharon and pull it leaf from leaf, and lay the leaves in the jar of memory and you shall find each leaf most fragrant long afterwards, filling the house with perfume.

This very day we remember times of refreshing enjoyed at the Lord's Table still delightful as we reflect upon them. Jesus is lovely in the bud as well as when full blown. You admire the rose quite as much when it is but a bud as when it bursts forth into perfect development. And I think Christ, to you, my Beloved, in the first blush of your piety, was not one whit less sweet than He is now. Jesus full blown, in our riper experience, has lost none of His excellence. When we shall see Him fully blown in the garden of Paradise, shall we not count it to be our highest Heaven to gaze upon Him forever? Christ is so lovely that He needs no beautifying.

When I hear men trying to speak of Him with polished sentences which have been revised, and re-revised upon their manuscripts, I would ask them why they need to paint the rose of Sharon and what they think they are doing in seeking to enamel the lily of the valleys? Hold up Christ Crucified, and He Himself is beautiful enough without our paint and tinsel! Let the roughest tongue speak sincerely of Him in the most broken but honest accents and Jesus Himself is such a radiant jewel that the setting will be of small consequence! He is so glorious that He is "Most adorned when unadorned the most." May we ever feel thus concerning Him, and if we are tempted to display our powers of oratory when we have to speak of Him, let us say, "Down, busy Pride, and let Christ rule, and let Christ be seen." He needs no help from you.

He is so lovely, again, that He satisfies the highest taste of the most educated spirit to the fullest. The greatest amateur in perfumes is quite satisfied with the rose, and I should think that no man of taste will ever be able to criticize the lily and laugh at its form. Now, when the soul has arrived at her highest pitch of true taste she shall still be content with Christ. No, she shall be the better able to appreciate Him! In the world's history we are supposed to have arrived at an age of taste, when color and form are much regarded. I must confess I think it a gaudy, tasteless age, and the fashion of the day is staring, vulgar, childish, and depraved.

Bright and glittering colors, antique, grotesque forms are much sought after—and men must introduce their chosen fineries and fopperies into their worship— supposing that it is comely to worship God with silks, and laces, and ribbons, and gilt, and tinsel, and I know not what of trumpery besides. Just as the harlot of Babylon arrayed herself in pearls and fine linen, and purple, and silk, and scarlet, even so do her imitators adorn themselves! As for us, my Brothers and Sisters, the beauty of Christ is such that if we go into a barn to worship, we are quite as satisfied as though it were a cathedral with grand arches and glowing windows!

Such is the beauty of Christ in our eyes that we are quite content to hear of Him without the pealing organ and the swell of Gregorian chants! And we are even satisfied though there should be no display of taste, nothing sensuous and scenic, nothing to please the eye or charm the ear. Jesus alone affords our minds all that delightful architecture, poetry, and music could profess to give! And when our soul gets near to Him, she looks upon all outward adornments as mere child's toys fit to amuse the rattle-brains of this poor idiot world—vain trinkets to men in Christ Jesus, who by reason of use have had their senses exercised and learned to delight in nobler things than those in which the swine of this earth delight themselves! God give you to know that if you want beauty, Jesus is Sharon's rose! If you want spotless charms to delight your true taste, He is the lily of the valleys.

Dwelling for another minute on this subject, let me remark that our Lord Jesus Christ deserves all that He has said of Himself. First, in His Divine Glory. The Glory of Christ as God—who shall write about it? The first-born sons of light desire to gaze into this vision but feel that their eyes are unable to endure the excess of light. He is God over all, blessed forever. Concerning Christ I may say that the heavens are not pure in His sight, and He charged His angels with folly. Nothing is great, nothing is excellent but God, and Christ is God! O roses and lilies, where are you now?

Our Lord deserves these praises, again, in His perfection of Manhood. He is like ourselves, but in Him was no sin. "The prince of this world comes, but has nothing in Me." Throughout the whole of His biography, there is not a fault. Let us write as carefully as we will after the copy, we still blot and blur the pages—but in Him there is no mistake. His life is so wonderfully perfect that even those who have denied His Deity have been astounded at it—and have bowed down before the majesty of His holiness. You roses of ardent love, and you lilies of purest holiness, where are you now when we compare you with this perfect man?

He deserves this commendation, too, in His editorial qualifications. Since His blood has washed us from all our sins, we talk no more of the red roses, for what can they do to purify the soul? Since His righteousness has made us accepted in the Beloved, we will speak no more of spotless lilies, for what are these? He deserves all this praise, too, in His reigning Glory. He has a Glory which His Father has given Him as a reward in the power of which He sits down at the right hand of God forever and ever, and shall soon come to judge the world in righteousness, and the people with equity. Beloved, when I think of the pompous appearance when He shall descend a second time in splendor upon the earth, I say again, you roses, your radiant beauties are utterly eclipsed, and you lilies, your snow-white purity is forgotten, I can scarcely discern you!

O fair flowers of earth, you are lost in the blaze of the Great White Throne, and in the flames of fire that shall go before the Judge of All to prepare His way! View the Lord Jesus in any way you please—all that He Himself can say concerning Himself He richly deserves—and therefore glory be unto His name forever and ever, and let the whole earth say, Amen.

III. I shall now conduct you to a third consideration, namely, THE INFLUENCE OF THIS COMMENDATION UPON US. Christ desires our loftiest thoughts of Himself and His desires are for our good. O my Beloved, I wish time would stay its wing a moment or two so that I might urge upon you that with all your hearts you would second the endeavors of Christ to labor after holy elevated thoughts concerning Himself since He desires them for you.

And if you ask me how you are to attain them, let me aid you a minute. Think of the ruin of this world till Christ came into it! I think I see in vision a howling wilderness, a great and terrible desert like the Sahara. I perceive nothing in it to relieve the eyes. All around I am wearied with a vision of hot and arid sand strewn with thousands of bleaching skeletons of wretched men who have expired in anguish, having lost their way in the pitiless waste. O God, what a sight! How horrible! A sea of sand without a boundary and without an oasis—a cheerless graveyard for a race forlorn!

But what is that I see? All of a sudden, upspringing from the scorching sand I see a root, a branch, a plant of renown! And as it grows, it buds! The bud expands—it is a rose, and at its side a lily bows its modest head—and miracle of miracles—as the fragrance of those flowers is diffused in the desert air I perceive that wilderness is transformed into a fruitful field, and all around it blossoms unlimited! The glory of Lebanon is given unto it! The excellency of Carmel and Sharon! Call it not Sahara, call it Paradise! Speak not of it any longer as the valley of death, for where I saw the skeletons bleaching in the sun, I see a resurrection—and up spring the dead, a mighty army, full of life immortal! You can understand the vision. Christ is the Rose which has changed the scene.

If you would have great thoughts of Christ think of your own ruin. Yonder I behold you cast out an infant, unwashed, defiled with your own blood, too foul to be looked upon except by beasts of prey! And what is this that has been cast into your bosom, and which lying there has suddenly made you fair and lovely? A rose has been thrown into your bosom by a Divine hand, and for its sake you have been pitied and cared for by Divine Providence. You are washed and cleaned from your defilement, you are adopted into Heaven's family, the fair seal of love is upon your forehead and the ring of faithfulness is on your hand. You are a prince unto God—though just now you were a castaway orphan.

O prize the rose, the putting of which into your bosom has made you what you are! Consider your daily need of this rose. You live in the pestilential air of this earth—take Christ away—you die. Christ is the daily food of your spirit. You know, Believer, that you are utterly powerless without your Lord. O prize Him, then, in proportion to the necessities you receive from Him! As you cannot even pray or think an acceptable thought apart from His Presence, I beseech you press Him to your bosom as the Beloved of your soul. You are like a branch cut off and withered—thrown outside the garden gate to be burnt as are the noxious weeds—apart from Him. But when you are near Him you bring forth fruit unto the glory of God. Praise Christ, I say, then, after the rate of the needs that you have received from Him.

Think, Beloved, of the estimation of Christ beyond the skies, in the land where things are measured by the right standard, where men are no longer deceived by the delusions of earth. Think how God esteems the Only Begotten, His unspeakable gift to us. Consider what the angels think of Him as they count it their highest honor to veil their faces at His feet. Consider what the blood-washed think of Him as day without night they sing His well-deserved praises with glad voices. Remember how you yourself have sometimes esteemed Him! There have been happy hours when you would freely have given your eyes and felt you cared no longer for the light of earth's brightest days, for your soul's eyes would serve you well enough if you could forever be favored with the same clear sight of Christ!

Have there not been moments when the chariots of Amminadib seemed but poor dragging things compared with the wheels of your soul when Jesus ravished your heart with His celestial embrace? Estimate Him today as you did then, for He is the same, though you are not. Think of Him today as you will think of Him in the hour of death, and in the day of judgment when none but Jesus can help to keep your soul alive. The great King has made a banquet and He has proclaimed to all the world that none shall enter but those who bring with them the fairest flower that blooms. The spirits of men advance to the gate by the thousands and they bring, each one, the flower which they think the best.

But in droves they are driven from His Presence and enter not into the banquet! Some bear in their hand the deadly nightshade of superstition, or carry the flaunting poppies of Rome—but these are not dear to the King—the bearers are shut out of the pearly gates. My soul, have you gathered the Rose of Sharon? Do you wear the Lily of the Valley in your bosom constantly? If so, when you come up to the gates of Heaven you will know its value, for you have only to show this and the porter will open the gate! Not for a moment will he deny the admission, for to that Rose the porter opens.

You shall find your way, with this Rose in your hand, up to the Throne of God Himself, for Heaven itself possess nothing which excels the Rose of Sharon! And of all the flowers that bloom in Paradise there is none that can rival the Lily of the Valleys. Get Calvary's blood-red Rose into your hand by faith and wear it. By communion preserve it. By daily watchfulness make it your All in All and you shall be blessed beyond all bliss—happy beyond a dream! So be it yours forever.

IV. Lastly, I shall close by asking you to make CONFESSIONS SUGGESTED BY MY TEXT. I will not make them for you, and therefore need not detain you from your homes. I will utter my own lamentation and leave you, every one apart, to do the same. I stand before this text of mine to blush, this morning, and to weep while I acknowledge my ungrateful behavior.

"My Lord, I am truly ashamed to think that I have not gazed more upon You. I know, and in my heart believe that You are the sum total of all beauty. Yet must I sorrowfully lament that my eyes have been gadding abroad to look after other beauties. My thoughts have been deluded with imaginary excellencies in the creatures, and I have meditated but little upon Yourself. Alas, my Lord, I confess still further that I have not possessed and enjoyed You as I ought. When I might have been with You all day and all night, I have been roving here and there, and forgetting my resting place. I have not been careful to welcome my Beloved and to retain His company. I have stirred Him up by my sins, and have driven Him away by my lukewarmness.

"I have given Him cold lodgings and slender hospitality within the chambers of my heart. I have not held Him fast, neither have I pressed Him to abide with me as I ought to have done. All this I must confess and mourn that I am not more ashamed while confessing it. Moreover, my good Lord, although I know Your great sacrifice for me might well have chained my heart forever to Your altar (and O that You had done so!) I must acknowledge that I have not been a living sacrifice as I should have been. I have not been as fascinated by the luster of Your beauty as I should have been. O that all my heart's rooms had been occupied by You, and by You alone!

"Would God my soul were as the coals in the furnace, all ablaze, and not a single particle of me left unconsumed by the delightful flames of Your love! I must also confess, my Lord, that I have not spoken of You as I should have done. Albeit I have had many opportunities, yet I have not praised You at the rate which You deserve. I have given You at best but a poor, stammering, chilly tongue when I should have spoken with the fiery zeal of a seraph."

These are my confessions; Brothers and Sisters, what are yours? If you have none to make, if you can justly claim to have done all that you should have done to your Beloved, I envy you! But I think there is not a man here who will dare to say this. I am sure you have all had falls, and slips, and shortcomings, with regard to Him. Well, then, come humbly to Jesus at once! He will forgive you readily, for He does not soon take offense at His spouse. He may sometimes speak sharp words to her because He loves her, but His heart is always true, and faithful, and tender. He will forgive the past! He will receive you at this moment! Yes, this *moment* He will display Himself to you!

If you will but open the door, He will enter into immediate fellowship with you, for He says, "Behold, I stand at the door and knock: if any man hears My voice, and opens the door, I will come in to him, and sup with him, and he with Me." O Christ, our Lord, our heart is open! Come in, and go out no more forever. Whoever believes on the Son has everlasting life." Sinner, believe and live!

UNDER THE APPLE TREE

DELIVERED BY C. H. SPURGEON,
AT THE METROPOLITCAN TABERNACLE, NEWINGTON.

*"I sat down under his shadow
with great delight, and his fruit
was sweet to my taste."*

Solomon's Song 2:3.

CHRIST *known should be Christ used*. The spouse knew her Beloved to be like a fruit-bearing tree and at once she sat down under His shadow and fed upon His fruit. It is a pity that we know so much about Christ and yet enjoy Him so little. May our experience keep pace with our knowledge and may that experience be composed of a practical using of our Lord. Jesus casts a shadow, let us sit under it. Jesus yields fruit; let us taste the sweetness of it. Depend upon it that the way to learn more is to use what you know and, moreover, the way to learn a Truth of God thoroughly is to learn it *experimentally*. You know a Doctrine beyond all fear of contradiction when you have proved it for yourself by personal test and trial. The bride in the Song as good as says, "I am certain that my Beloved casts a shadow, for I have sat under it, and I am persuaded that He bears sweet fruit, for I have tasted of it." The best way of demonstrating the power of Christ to save is to trust in Him and be, yourself, saved by Him—and of all those who are sure of the Divinity of our holy faith, there are none so certain as those who feel its Divine Power upon themselves! You may reason yourself into a belief of the Gospel and you may, by further reasoning, keep yourself orthodox—but a personal trial and an inward knowing of the Truth are incomparably the best evidences. If Jesus is as an apple tree among the trees of the woods, do not stay away from Him, but sit under His shadow and taste His fruit! He is a Savior—do not believe that fact and yet remain unsaved. As far as Christ is known to you, so far make use of Him! Is not this sound common sense?

We would further remark that *we are at liberty to make every possible use of Christ.* Shadow and fruit may both be enjoyed. Christ, in His Infinite condescension exists for needy souls. Oh, let us say it over again! It is a bold word, but it is true—as Christ Jesus our Lord exists for the benefit of His people! A Savior only exists to save. A physician lives to heal. The Good Shepherd lives, yes, dies for His sheep! Our Lord Jesus Christ has wrapped us about His heart—we are intimately interwoven with all His offices, with all His honors, with all His traits of Character, with all that He has done and with all that He has yet to do! The sinners' Friend lives for sinners and sinners may have Him and use Him to the uttermost! He is as free to us as the air we breathe! What are fountains for but that the thirsty may drink? What is the harbor for but that storm-tossed ships may there find refuge? What is Christ for, but that poor guilty ones like ourselves may come to Him and look and live—and afterwards may have all our needs supplied out of His fullness?

We have thus the door set open for us and we pray that the Holy Spirit may help us to enter in while we notice in the text two things which we pray that you may enjoy to the fullest. First, *the heart's rest in Christ*—"I sat down under His shadow with great delight." And secondly, *the heart's refreshment in Christ*—"His fruit was sweet to my taste."

I. To begin with, we have here THE HEART'S REST IN CHRIST. To set this forth, let us notice the character of the person who uttered this sentence. She who said, "I sat down under His shadow with great delight," was *one who had known before what weary travel meant and, therefore, valued rest*. The man who has never labored knows nothing of the sweetness of repose. The loafer who has eaten bread he never earned, from whose brow there never oozed a drop of honest sweat does not deserve rest—and knows not what it is. It is to the laboring man that rest is sweet! And when at last we come, toil-worn with many miles of weary plodding, to a shaded place where we may comfortably "sit down"— then are we filled with delight!

The spouse had been seeking her Beloved, and in looking for Him she had asked where she was likely to find Him. "Tell me," she says, "O You whom my soul loves, where You feed, where You make Your flock to rest at noon." He told her to go and seek Him by the footsteps of the flock. She did go her way, but after a while she came to this resolve—"I will *sit down* under His shadow." Many of you have been sorely wearied with going your way to find peace. Some of you tried ceremonies and multiplied them, and the priest came to your help, but he mocked your hearts' distress. Others of you sought by various systems of *thought* to come to an anchorage. But tossed from billow to billow, you found no rest upon the seething sea of speculation. More of you tried by your good works to go in rest to your consciences. You multiplied your prayers, you poured out floods of tears. You hoped by alms-giving and by the like that some merit might accrue to you and that your heart might feel acceptance with God, and so have rest. You toiled and toiled, like the men that were in the vessel with Jonah when they rowed hard to bring their ship to land, but could not, for the sea worked and was tempestuous. There was no escape for you that way and so you were driven to another way—even to rest in Jesus! My heart looks back to the time when I was under a sense of sin and sought with all my soul to find peace, but could not discover it, high or low, in any place beneath the sky! Yet when—

"I saw One hanging on a tree"—

as the Substitute for sin, then my heart sat down under His shadow with great delight! My heart reasoned thus with herself—did Jesus suffer in *my* place? Then I shall not suffer! Did He bear my sin? Then I do not bear it! Did

God accept His Son as my Substitute? Then He will never smite *me*! Was Jesus acceptable with God as my Sacrifice? Then what contents the Lord may well enough content me, so I will go no further, but "sit down under His shadow," and enjoy a delightful rest!

She who said, "I sat down under His shadow with great delight," could appreciate shade, for she had been sunburned. This was her exclamation, "Look not upon me, because I am black, because the sun has looked upon me." She knew what heat meant, what the burning sun meant and, therefore, shade was pleasant to her. You know nothing about the deliciousness of shade till you travel in a thoroughly hot country—then you are delighted with it! Did you ever feel the heat of Divine Wrath? Did the great Sun—that Sun without variableness or shadow of a turning—ever dart His hottest rays upon you—the rays of His holiness and justice? Did you cower down beneath the scorching beams of that great Light of God and say, "We are consumed by Your anger"? If you have ever felt *that*, you have found it a very blessed thing to come under the shadow of Christ's atoning Sacrifice! A shadow, you know, is cast by a body coming between us and the light and heat—and our Lord's most blessed body has come between us and the scorching sun of Divine Justice, so that we sit under the shadow of His mediation with great delight!

And now, if any other sun begins to scorch us, we fly to our Lord. If domestic troubles, or business cares, or satanic temptations, or inward corruptions oppress us, we hasten to Jesus' shadow to hide under Him and there "sit down" in the cool refreshment with great delight! The interposition of our blessed Lord is the cause of our inward quiet. The sun cannot scorch *me*, for it scorched *Him*. My troubles need not trouble me, for He has taken my troubles and I have left them in His hands. "I sat down under His shadow."

Mark well these two things concerning the spouse. She knew what it was to be weary and she knew what it was to be sunburned—and just in proportion as you, also, know these two things, your valuation of Christ will rise! You who have never lingered under the wrath of God have never prized the Savior! Water is of small value in this land of brooks and rivers, and so you commonly sprinkle the roads with it. But I guarantee you that if you were making a day's march over burning sand, a cup of cold water would be worth a king's ransom! And so to thirsty souls Christ is precious, but to none beside!

Now, when the spouse was sitting down, restful and delighted, *she was overshadowed*. She says, "I sat down under His shadow." I do not know a more delightful state of mind than to feel quite overshadowed by our Beloved Lord. Here is my black sin, but there is His precious blood overshadowing my sin and hiding it forever! Here is my condition by nature, an enemy to

God, but He who reconciled me to God by His blood has overshadowed that, also, so that I forget that I was once an enemy in the joy of being now a friend! I am very weak, but He is strong and His strength overshadows my feebleness. I am very poor, but He has all riches and His riches overshadow my poverty. I am most unworthy, but He is so worthy that if I use His name, I shall receive as much as if I were worthy! His worthiness overshadows my unworthiness! It is very precious to put the truth the other way and say—If there is anything good in me, it is not good when I compare myself with Him, for His goodness quite eclipses and overshadows it! Can I say that I love Him? So I do, but I hardly dare call it love, for His love overshadows it. Did I suppose that I *served* Him? So I would, but my poor service is not worth mentioning in comparison with what He has done for me! Did I think I had any degree of holiness? I must not deny that His Spirit works in me—but when I think of His immaculate life and all His Divine perfections, where am I? What am I? Have you not sometimes felt this? Have you not been so overshadowed and hidden under your Lord that you became as nothing? I know what it is to feel that if I die in a workhouse, it does not matter as long as my Lord is glorified. Mortals may cast out my name as evil, if they like, but what does it matter since His dear name shall one day be printed in stars across the sky? Let Him overshadow me—I delight that it should be so!

The spouse tells us that when she became quite overshadowed, then *she felt great delight*. Great "I" never has great delight, for it cannot bear to acknowledge a greater than itself, but the humble Believer finds his delight in being overshadowed by his Lord! In the shade of Jesus we have more delight than in any fancied light of our own. The spouse had *great* delight. I trust that you Christian people have great delight. But if not, you ought to ask yourselves whether you really are the people of God. I like to see a cheerful countenance—yes, and to hear of raptures in the hearts of those who are God's saints. There are people who seem to think that religion and gloom are married and must never be divorced. Pull down the blinds on Sunday and darken the rooms! If you have a garden or a rose in bloom, try to forget that there are such beauties—are you not to serve God as dolorously as you can? Put your book under your arm and crawl to your place of worship in as mournful a manner as if you were being marched to the whipping-post! Act thus if you will, but give me that religion which cheers my heart, fires my soul and fills me with enthusiasm and delight—for that is likely to be the religion of Heaven—and it agrees with the experience of the Inspired Song!

Although I trust that we know what delight means, I question if we have enough of it to describe ourselves as *sitting down* in the enjoyment of it. Do you give yourselves enough time to sit at Jesus' feet? *There* is the place of delight! Do you abide in it? Sit down under His shadow. "I have no leisure," cries one. Try and make a little. Steal it from your sleep if you cannot get it anywhere else. Grant leisure to your heart. It would be a great pity if a man never spent five minutes with his wife but was forced to be always hard at work. Why, that is slavery, is it not? Shall we not, then, have time to commune with our Best-Beloved? Surely, somehow or other, we can squeeze out a little season in which we shall have nothing else to do but to sit down under His shadow with great delight! When I take my Bible and need to feed on it for myself, I generally get to thinking about preaching upon the text and what I should say to you from it. This will not do! I must get away from that and forget that there is a Tabernacle, that I may sit personally at Jesus' feet! And, oh, there is an intense delight in being overshadowed by Him! He is near you and you know it. His dear Presence is as certainly with you as if you could see Him, for His influence surrounds you! Often have I felt as if Jesus leaned over me, as a friend might look over my shoulder. Although no cool shade comes over your brow, yet you may as much feel His shadow as if it did, for your heart grows calm—and if you have been wearied with the family, or troubled with the Church, or vexed with yourself—you come down from the chamber where you have seen your Lord and you feel braced for the battle of life—ready for its troubles and its temptations because you have seen the Lord!

"I sat down," she said, "under His shadow with *great delight*." How great that delight was she could not tell, but she sat down as one overpowered with it, needing to sit still under the load of bliss! I do not like to talk much about the secret delights of Christians because there are always some around us who do not understand our meaning. But I will venture to say this much—if worldlings could but even *guess* what are the secret joys of Believers, they would give their eyes to share them with us! We have troubles and we admit it. We expect to have them, but we have joys which are frequently excessive. We would not like that others should be witnesses of the delight which now and then tosses our soul into a very tempest of joy. You know what it means, do you not? When you have been quite alone with the heavenly Bridegroom, you wanted to tell the angels of the sweet love of Christ to you, a poor unworthy one! You even wished to teach the golden harps fresh music, for seraphs know not the heights and depths of Grace as you know them.

The spouse had a great delight—and we know that she had for this one reason—*she did not forget it*. This verse and the whole Song is a remembrance of what she had enjoyed. She says, "I sat down under His shadow." It may have been a month, it may have been years ago, but she had not forgotten it! The joys of fellowship with God are written in marble. "Engraved as in eternal brass" are memories of communion with Christ Jesus!

"Above fourteen years ago," says the Apostle, "I knew a man." Ah, it was worth remembering all those years! He had not told his delight, but he had kept it stored up. He says, "I knew a man in Christ above fourteen years ago, whether in the body, I cannot tell; or whether out of the body, I cannot tell: God knows," so great had his delights been! When we look back, we forget birthdays, holidays and bonfire-nights which we have spent after the manner of men, but we readily recall our times of fellowship with the Well-Beloved! We have known our Tabors, our times of transfiguration-fellowship and, like Peter, we remember when we were "with Him in the holy mount." Our head has leaned upon the Master's bosom and we can never forget the intense delight! Nor will we fail to put on record for the good of others the joys with which we have been indulged.

Now I leave this first part of the subject, only noticing how beautifully natural it is. There was a tree and she sat down under the shadow. There was nothing strained, nothing formal. So ought true piety always be consistent with common sense, with that which seems most fitting, most comely, most wise and most natural. There is Christ, we may enjoy Him—let us not despise the privilege!

II. The second part of our subject is THE HEART'S REFRESHMENT IN CHRIST. "His fruit was sweet to my taste." Here I will not enlarge, but give you thoughts in brief which you can beat out afterwards.

She did not feast upon the fruit of the tree till first she was under the shadow of it. There is no knowing the excellent things of Christ till you trust Him. Not a single sweet apple shall fall to the lot of those who are outside the shadow. Come and trust Christ—and then all that there is in Christ shall be enjoyed by you. O unbelievers, what blessings you miss! If you will but sit down under His shadow, you shall have all things. But if you will not, neither shall any good thing of Christ's be yours.

But as soon as she was under the shadow, then the fruit was all hers. "I sat down under His shadow," she says, and then, "His fruit was sweet to my taste." Do you believe in Jesus, Friend? Then Jesus Christ Himself is yours! And if you own the tree, you may as well eat the fruit. Since He Himself becomes yours altogether, then His redemption and the pardon that comes of it, His living power, His mighty intercession, the glories of His Second Advent and all that belong to Him are made over to you for your personal and present use and enjoyment! All things are yours since Christ is yours! Only mind that you imitate the spouse—*when she found that the fruit was hers, she ate it*. Copy her closely in this. It is a great fault in many Believers that they do not appropriate the promises and feed on them. Do not err as they do! Under the shadow, you have a right to eat the fruit. Deny not yourselves the sacred entertainment.

Now it would appear, as we read the text, that *she obtained this fruit without effort*. The proverb says, "He who would gain the fruit must climb the tree." But she did not climb, for she says, "I sat down under His shadow." I suppose the fruit dropped down to her. I know that it is so with us. We no longer spend our money for that which is not bread, and our labor for that which satisfies not—we sit under our Lord's shadow and we eat that which is good—and our soul delights itself in sweetness. Come, Christian, enter into the calm rest of faith by sitting down beneath the Cross and you shall be fed even to the fullest!

The spouse rested while feasting—she sat and ate. So, O true Believer, rest while you are feeding upon Christ. The spouse says, "I sat and I ate." Had she not told us, in the former chapter, that the King *sat* at His table? See how like the Church is to her Lord and the Believer to his Savior! We also sit down and we eat, even as the King does. Right royally are we entertained. His joy is in us and His peace keeps our hearts and minds!

Further, notice that *as the spouse fed upon this fruit, she had a relish for it*. It is not every palate that likes every fruit. Never dispute with other people about tastes of any sort, for agreement is not possible. That dainty which to one person is the most delicious, is to another nauseous. And if there was a competition as to which fruit is preferable to all the rest, there would probably be almost as many opinions as there are fruits! But blessed is he who has a relish for Christ Jesus! Dear Hearer, is He sweet to you? Then He is yours! There never was a heart that relished Christ but what Christ belonged to that heart! If you have been feeding on Him and He is sweet to you, go on feasting, for He who gave you a relish gives you Himself to satisfy your appetite!

What are the fruits which come from Christ? Are they not peace with God, renewal of heart, joy in the Holy Spirit, and love to the brethren? Are they not regeneration, justification, sanctification, adoption and all the blessings of the Covenant of Grace? And are they not each and all sweet to our taste? As we fed upon them, have we not said, "Yes, these things are pleasant, indeed. There are none like them—let us live upon them forevermore." Now sit down, sit down and feed. It seems a strange thing that we should have to persuade people to do that, but in a spiritual world, things are very different from what they are in the natural. In the case of most men, if you put a roast before them and a knife and fork, they do not need many arguments to persuade them to fall to! But I will tell you when they will not do it, and that is when they are full! And I will also tell you when they *will* do it, and that is when they are hungry. Even so, if your soul is weary after Christ the Savior, you will feed on Him. But if not, it is useless for me to preach to you, or bid you come. However, you who are there, sitting under His shadow, may hear Him utter these words, "Eat, O Friend. Drink, yes, drink abundantly." You cannot have too much of these good things—the more of Christ, the better the Christian!

We know that the spouse feasted herself right heartily with this food from the Tree of Life, for *in latter days, she wanted more.* Will you kindly read on in the 4th verse? The verse which contains our text describes, as it were, her first love to her Lord, her country love, her rustic love. She went to the woods and she found Him there like an apple tree and she enjoyed Him as one relishes a ripe apple in the country. But she grew in Grace—she learned more of her Lord and she found that her Best-Beloved was King. I should not wonder but what she learned the Doctrine of the Second Advent, for then she began to sing, "He brought me to the banqueting house," as much as to say—He did not merely let me know Him out in the fields as the Christ in His humiliation, but He brought me into the royal palace and, since He is a King, He brought forth a banner with His own brave escutcheon and He waved it over me while I was sitting at the table—and the motto of that banner was LOVE.

She grew very full of this. It was such a grand thing to find a great Savior, a triumphant Savior, an exalted Savior—but it was too much for her and she became sick of soul with the excessive glory of what she had learned. And do you see what her heart craves for? She longs for her first simple joys, those countrified delights. "Comfort me with apples," she says. Nothing but the old joys will revive her! Did you ever feel like that? I have been satiated with delight in the love of Christ as a glorious, exalted Savior when I have seen Him riding on His white horse and going forth conquering and to conquer. I have been overwhelmed when I have beheld Him in the midst of the Throne of God with all the brilliant assembly of angels and archangels adoring Him. And my thoughts have gone forward to the day when He shall descend with all the pomp of God—and make all kings and princes shrink into nothingness before the Infinite Majesty of His Glory! Then I have felt as though I must fall at His feet as dead at the sight of Him and I have needed somebody to come and tell me over again the old, old story of how He died in order that I might be saved! His Throne overpowers me! Let me gather fruit from His Cross! Bring me apples from "the tree" again. I am awe-struck while in the palace! Let me get away to the woods again. Give me an apple plucked from the tree, such as I have given out to boys and girls in His family, such an apple as this, "Come unto Me, all you that labor and are heavy laden, and I will give you rest." Or this, "This Man receives sinners." Give me a promise from the basket of the Covenant! Give me the simplicity of Christ—let me be a child and feast on apples, again, if Jesus is the apple tree! I would gladly go back to Christ on the tree in my place, Christ overshadowing me, Christ feeding me. This is the happiest state to live in! Lord, give us these apples evermore!

You remember the old story we told years ago of Jack the huckster, who used to sing—

"I'm a poor sinner, and nothing at all,
But Jesus Christ is my All-in-All."

Those who knew him were astonished at his constant composure. They had a world of doubts and fears and so they asked him why he never doubted. "Well," he said, "I can't doubt but what I am a poor sinner, and nothing at all, for I know that, and feel it every day. But why should I doubt that Jesus Christ is my All-in-All, for He says He is?" "Oh," said his questioner, "I have my ups and downs." "I don't," said Jack, "I can never go up, for I am a poor sinner and nothing at all. And I cannot go down, for Jesus Christ is my All-in-All." He wanted to join the Church, and they said he must tell his experience. He said, "All my experience is that I am a poor sinner, and nothing at all, and Jesus Christ is my All-in-All." "Well," they said, "when you come before the Church meeting, the minister may ask you questions." "I can't help it," said Jack, "all I know I will tell you. And this is all I know—

'I'm a poor sinner, and nothing at all,
But Jesus Christ is my All-in-All.'"

He was admitted into the Church and continued with the brethren, walking in holiness. But that was still all his experience and you could not get him beyond it. "Why," said one Brother, "I sometimes feel so full of Grace, I feel so advanced in sanctification, that I begin to be very happy." "I never do," said Jack. "I am a poor sinner, and nothing at all." "But then," said the other, "I go down again and think I am not saved because I am not as sanctified as I used to be." "But I never doubt my salvation," said Jack, "because Jesus Christ is my All-in-All and He never alters." That simple story is grandly instructive, for it sets forth a plain man's faith in a plain salvation. It is the likeness of a soul under the apple tree resting in the shade and feasting on the fruit!

Now, at this time, I want you to think of Jesus, not as a Prince, but as an apple tree! And when you have done this, I pray you to *sit down under His shadow*. It is not much to do. Any child, when it is hot, can sit down in a shadow. I want you, next, to feed on Jesus. Any simpleton can eat apples when they are ripe upon the tree. Come and take Christ, then. You who never came before, come now! Come and welcome! You who have come often and have entered into the palace, and are reclining at the banqueting table—you lords and peers of Christianity—come to the common woods and to the common apple tree, where poor saints are shaded and fed. You had better come under the apple tree like poor sinners such as I am, and be once more shaded with branches and comforted with apples, or else you may faint beneath the palace glories! The best of saints are never better than when they eat their first fare and are comforted with the apples which were their first Gospel feast!

The Lord Himself bring forth His own sweet fruit to you.
Amen.

LOVE JOYING IN LOVE

A SHORT ADDRESS TO A FEW FRIENDS
AT MENTONE, AT THE BREAKING OF BREAD,
ON LORD'S-DAY AFTERNOON,
JANUARY 9, 1887

BY C. H. SPURGEON

*"I am come into my garden, my sister,
my spouse: I have gathered my myrrh
with my spice; I have eaten my honeycomb
with my honey; I have drunk my wine
with my milk: eat, O friends; drink, yea,
drink abundantly, O beloved."*

Song of Solomon 5:1

No sooner does the spouse say, "Let my Beloved come into His garden," than her Lord answers, "I am come into My garden." "Before they call, I will answer; and while they are yet speaking, I will hear." When we desire our Lord Jesus to come to us, He has already come, in a measure—our desire is the *result* of His coming! He meets us in all our desires, for He waits to be gracious. Our, "Come," is no sooner uttered than it is lost in His, "Behold, I come quickly!"

When we perceive that the Bridegroom has come, we perceive, also, that He has done exactly what He was asked to do. How cheering to find that our mind is in harmony with His mind! Our heart says, "Let my Beloved come into His garden and eat His pleasant fruits." His heart replies, "I have gathered My myrrh with My spice; I have eaten My honeycomb with My honey; I have drunk My wine with My milk." "Delight yourself also in the Lord and He shall give you the desires of your heart." The Lord Jesus makes the desires of His saints to be the foreshadowing of His own actions—"The secret of the Lord is with them that fear Him." His secret counsel is made known in the believing soul by desires inspired by the Holy Spirit.

Note well that the Bridegroom kindly takes to Himself as His own all that is in the garden. His souse spoke of, "His pleasant fruits," and He acknowledges the least and most homely of them to be His own. He repeats the possessive particle—"My." "*My* myrrh, *My* spice, *My* honeycomb, *My* honey, *My* wine, *My* milk." He disdains nothing which the garden of His bride produces. He is fond on the notion of joint-heirship, even as in another place He said, "My Father, and your Father, My God, and your God." Let us also value the personal possessive pronouns—the sweetness of the promises lies in them. These are our arms with which we embrace the promises.

Beloved Brothers and Sisters in Christ Jesus, is it not charming to see our Lord appropriating us—all that we are, all that we have, all that grows within us—and all the varied form of His Grace which are the outcome of

His own work within our hearts? Within us, certain things are bitter, but wholesome—and He says, "My myrrh." Some things are sweet, though homely—and He says, "My honey." Some things are of a rarer sort and He says, "My spice"—while others are commonplace enough—and He says, "My milk." Our Lord takes no exception to any one of the true growths of the garden, whether it is myrrh or milk. And He asks for nothing more than the garden may be expected to yield. He is content without the butter of cows, or flesh of fed beasts—satisfying Himself with honey fresh from the hive.

I note, with much delight, that matters which seem inconsistent with perfection are not refused by the heavenly Bridegroom. As the Lord did not refuse for an offering the leavened cakes of the first fruits, so in this instance He says, "I have eaten My honeycomb with My honey." The honey would be purer without the comb, but as it is incident thereto, He takes the one with the other. He graciously accepts not only our heart's desire, but the very mode in which our weakness works towards that desire! It is as if He delighted in the words of our prayers as well as in the *essence* of our prayers and prized the notes of our songs as well as the meaning of them. Yes, I believe our Lord puts our tears as well as our sorrows into His bottle and hears our groans as well as our desires! The honeycomb which contains the honey is precious to Him! After He had risen from the grave, He ate a piece of honeycomb and I doubt not that He had a reason for choosing that food—sweet gathered from sweets, yet not without wax. Our Lord accepts our services without nicely noting and critically rejecting the infirmity which goes with them.

I note, also, that He, Himself, gathers what He enjoys—"I have gathered My myrrh with My spice." Many a holy thing which we have not in detail offered to Him in set form, He knows to have been given in the gross and so He takes with His own hands what He knows we have, by a comprehensive covenant, made over to Him. How sweetly does He fill up our blanks and believe in our consecration, even when we do not repeat the form of it!

Moreover, He makes mixtures out of our fruits, for He gathers myrrh with balsam and drinks wine with milk, thus taking the rarer with the more common. He knows how to make holy compounds out of the Grace of His people, thus increasing their excellence. He is the best judge of what is admirable and He is the best fashioner and mixer of character—He is using His skill upon us. Often by our mingled experiences He accomplishes an increase of virtue in us. Some Graces are the result of work and wisdom, as wine which much be trod from the grapes. Others are natural, like milk which flows from living fountains without art of man. But the Lord accepts them both and so combines them that they are pleasant to Him to a high degree. Simple faith and experimental prudence make up a sacred milk and wine—and the like may be seen in rapturous love and calm patience which blend most deliciously! The Lord loves us and makes the most of us. He is pleased with all that is the true produce of His Grace and finds no faults with it—on the contrary, He says, "I have eaten My honeycomb with My honey."

Having made these observations upon the Lord's fulfilling the prayer of the spouse, I should like to deliver the following remarks upon the text—

It is evident that *the Lord Jesus is made happy by us.* These poetical sentences must mean that He values the Graces and works of His people. He gathers their myrrh and spice because He values them! He eats and drinks the honey and the milk because they are pleasant to Him. It is a wonderful thought that the Lord Jesus Christ has joy in us! We cost Him anguish, even unto death, and now He finds a *reward* in us. This may seem a small thing to an unloving mind, but it may well ravish the heart which adores the Well-Beloved! Can it be true that we afford *joy* to the Son of God, the Prince Emmanuel? The King has been held in the galleries! He has been charmed by us! Our first repentance made Him call together His friends and His neighbors. The first gleam of faith He ever saw in us made His heart rejoice and all that He has seen in us ever since of His own image, worked by His Grace, has caused Him to see of the travail of His soul! Never has a farmer taken such pleasure in the growth of his choice plants as our Lord has taken in us! "The Lord takes pleasure in them that fear Him; in those that hope in His mercy." That is a thought to be rolled under the tongue as a sweet morsel! Yes, the Lord's Church is His Hephzibah, for, He says, "My delight is in her."

The second thought is that *the Lord Jesus will not and cannot be happy by Himself—He will have us share with Him*. Note how the words run—"I have eaten." "Eat, O friends!" "I have drunk." "Drink, yes, drink abundantly, O Beloved." His union with His people is so close that His joy is in them, that their joy may be full. He cannot be alone in His joy! That verse of our quaint hymn is always true—

> **"And this I do find, we two are so joined,**
> **He'll not be in Glory and leave me behind."**

He will not be happy anywhere without us. He will not eat without our eating and He will not drink without our drinking. Does He not say this in other words in the Revelation—"If any man hears My voice and opens the door, I will come in to him and will sup with him, and He with me"? The inter-communion is complete—the enjoyment is for *both*. To make our Lord Jesus happy, we must also be happy. How can the Bridegroom rejoice if His bride is sad? How can the Head be content if the members pine? At this table of fellowship, His chief concern is that we eat and drink. "Take, eat," He says. And again, "Drink you, all of it." I think I hear Him now say—"I have eaten and I have drunk. And although I will drink no more of the fruit of the vine until that day that I drink it new in the Kingdom of God; yet eat you, O friends: drink, yes, drink abundantly, O Beloved!" Thus we have seen, first, that Christ is made happy by us and, secondly, that He insists upon our sharing His joy with Him.

If we have already enjoyed happy fellowship with Him, *the Lord Jesus calls upon us to be still more happy.* Though we may say that we have eaten, He will again say, "Eat, O friends!" He presses you to renew, repeat and increase your participation with Him. It is true we have drunk out of the chalice of His love, but He again invites us, saying, "Drink, yes, drink abundantly, O Beloved!" Of other wines it would be bad to say, "Drink abundantly," but of this wine the Lord says, with an emphasis, "Drink abundantly, O Beloved!" Oh, for Grace to renew all former enjoyments with greater zest and deeper intensity! It has been sweet even to taste and sip—what must it be to eat and *drink abundantly*?

Must it not mean that though we know the Lord Jesus, we should try to know more of Him, yes, to know *all* that can be known of that love which passes knowledge? Should we not labor to realize more of HIM, taking in the whole Truth of God concerning His Person and love by meditation, contemplation, understanding and reverent simplicity? Let nothing lie by—let us eat and drink all the stores of the banquet of love!

As the mouth with which we eat is flesh, does not the Savior seem to cry, "Believe on Me. Trust Me. Confide in Me abundantly"? Eat and drink with large appetite, by receiving into your heart's belief all that can be received. Oh, for Grace to appropriate a whole Christ and all the love, the Grace, the Glory that is laid up in Him!

Does it not also mean have greater enjoyment of Divine things? Partake of them without stint. Do not restrict yourself as though you could go too far in feeding upon the Lord Jesus! Do not be afraid of being too happy in the Lord, or of being too sure of His salvation, or of having too much assurance, or too much devout emotion! Dread not the excitements which come from fellowship with Christ! Do not believe that the love of Jesus can be too powerfully felt in the soul. Permit the full sweep and current of holy joy in the Lord to carry you away—it will be safe to yield to it. "Rejoice in the Lord always and again, I say, Rejoice."

Beloved, let us now take our fill of Christ. Since we believe, let us believe more unreservedly! If we enjoy, let us enjoy more thoroughly! If we have life, let us have it more abundantly. In this case we may eat and our soul shall live! We may drink and not only forget our misery, but drink again and enter into bliss! Our Lord beckons us from the shore to the sea. He calls us from the lower seat to come up higher. He would have us more glad, stronger, fuller, holier! He presses the provisions of His love upon us, like a host whose joy lies in seeing all his guests feasting. Do not hold back! Be not satisfied with little believing, scant enjoying and cool feeling—but let us enter fully into the joy of our Lord!

True, we are unworthy, but He invites us! We shall be wise to yield to His loving pressure. We may not have such another feast, just yet, and possibly we may have to go for 40 days into the wilderness on the strength of this meal. Therefore let us keep the feast heartily! Our Lord, in His invitation, challenges our friendship and our love. He says—"Eat, O *friends*!" Prove yourselves friends by being free at His table. "Drink, yes, drink abundantly, O *Beloved*!" If this is His way of testing us, let us not be slow in accepting it. Let us show our love by joying in Him as He joys in us! Amen.

MY GARDEN – HIS GARDEN

DELIVERED ON THURSDAY EVENING,
JULY 20TH, 1882
BY C. H. SPURGEON

AT THE METROPOLITAN TABERNACLE,
NEWINGTON

"Awake, O north wind; and come, thou south; blow upon my garden, that the spices thereof may flow out. Let my beloved come into his garden, and eat his pleasant fruits."

Song of Solomon 4:16

WHAT a difference there is between what the Believer was by nature and what the Grace of God has made him! Naturally, we were like the waste howling wilderness, like the desert which yields no healthy plant or verdure. It seemed as if we were given over to be like a salt land which is not inhabited—no good thing was in us, or could spring out of us. But now, as many of us as have known the Lord are transformed into gardens—our wilderness is made like Eden, our desert is changed into the garden of the Lord. "I will turn to you," said the Lord to the mountains of Israel when they were bleak and bare, "I will turn to you and you shall be tilled and sown." And this is exactly what He said to the barrenness of our nature. We have been enclosed by

Grace, we have been tilled and sown, we have experienced all the operations of the Divine Farmer. Our Lord Jesus said to His disciples, "My Father is the Farmer," and He has made us to be fruitful to His praise, full of sweetness where once there was no fruit and nothing that could give Him delight.

We are a garden, then, and in a garden there are flowers and fruit. And in every Christian's heart you will find the same evidences of culture and care—not in all, alike, for even gardens and fields vary in productiveness. In the good ground mentioned by our Lord in the parable of the sower, the good seed did not all bring forth a hundredfold, or even sixty-fold. There were some parts of the field where the harvest was as low as thirty-fold and I fear that there are some of the Lord's gardens which yield even less than that. Still, there are the fruits and there are the flowers in measure. There is a good beginning made wherever the Grace of God has undertaken the culture of our nature.

I. Now coming to our text, and thinking of Christians as the Lord's garden, I want you to observe, first, that THERE ARE SWEET SPICES IN BELIEVERS.

The text assumes, when it says, "Blow upon my garden, that the spices thereof may flow out," that there are, in the Lord's garden, sweet flowers that drip with honey, and all manner of delightful perfumes. There *are* such sweet spices within the Believer's heart—let us think of them for a few minutes and first, let me remind you of *the names of these sweet spices*.

For instance, there is *faith*. Is there anything out of Heaven sweeter than faith—the faith which trusts and clings, which believes and hopes, and declares that, though God shall slay it, yet will it trust in Him? In the Lord's esteem, faith is full of fragrance. He never delighted in the burning of bulls and the fat of fed beasts, but He always delighted in the faith which brought these things as types of the one great Sacrifice for sin. Faith is very dear to Him.

Then comes *love* and, again, I must ask—Is there to be found anywhere a sweeter spice than this—the love which loves God because He first loved us, the love which flows out to all the brotherhood, the love which knows no circle within which it can be bounded, but which loves the whole race of mankind and seeks to do them good? It is exceedingly pleasing to God to see love growing where once all was hate—and to see faith springing up in that very soul which was formerly choked with the thorns and briers of doubt and unbelief!

And there is also *hope* which is, indeed, an excellent Grace, a far-seeing Grace by which we behold Heaven and eternal bliss. There is such a fragrance about a God-given hope that this poor sin-stricken world seems to be cured by it. Wherever this living, lively hope comes, there men lift up their drooping heads and begin to rejoice in God their Savior. You do not need that I should go over all the list of Christian Graces and mention meekness, brotherly kindness, courage, uprightness, or the patience which endures so much from the hand of God—whatever Grace I might mention, it would not be difficult at once to convince you that there is a sweetness and a perfume about all Grace in the esteem of Him who created it—and it delights Him that it should flourish where once its opposite was found growing in the heart of man. These, then, are *some* of the saints' sweet spices.

Next, notice that *these sweet spices are delightful to God*. It is very wonderful that we should have within us anything in which God can take delight. Yet when we think of all the other wonders of His Grace, we need not marvel at all. The God who gave us faith may well be pleased with faith. The God who created love in such unlovely hearts as ours may well be delighted at His own creation. He will not despise the work of His own hands—rather will He be delighted with it and find sweet complacency therein. What an exaltation it is to us worms of the earth that there should ever be anything in us well-pleasing to God! Well did the Psalmist say, "What is man, that You are mindful of Him? And the son of man, that you visit Him?" But God *is* mindful of us and He *does* visit us! Of old, before Christ came into this world in human form, His delights were with the sons of men—much more is it so now that

He has taken their nature into Heaven, itself, and given to those sons of men His own Spirit to dwell within them! Let it ravish your heart with intense delight that though often you can take no complacency in yourself, but go with your head bowed down like a bulrush and cry, "Woe is me!" yet in that very cry of yours, God hears a note that is sweet and musical to His ears!

Blessed is *repentance*, with her teardrops in her eyes, sparkling like diamonds. God even takes delight in our longings after holiness and in our loathing of our own imperfections. Just as the father delights to see his child anxious to be on the best and most loving terms with him, so does God delight in us when we are crying after that which we have not yet reached—the perfection which shall make us to be fully like Himself! O Beloved, I do not know anything that fills my soul with such feelings of joy as does the reflection that I, even I, may yet be and do something that shall give delight to the heart of God, Himself! He has joy over one sinner that repents, though repentance is but an initial Grace—and when we go on from that to other Graces and take yet higher steps in the Divine life—we may be sure that His joy is in us and, therefore, our joy may well be full.

These spices of ours are not only delightful to God, but *they are healthy to man*. Every particle of faith that there is in the world is a sort of purifier. Wherever it goes, it has a tendency to kill that which is evil. In the spiritual sanitary arrangements which God made for this poor world, He put men of faith—and the faith of these men—into the midst of all this corruption to help to keep other men's souls alive, even as our Lord Jesus said to His disciples, "You are the salt of the earth." The sweet perfumes that flow out from the flowers which God cultivates in the garden of His Church are scattering spiritual health and sanity all around! It is a blessed thing that the Lord has provided these sweet spices to overpower and counteract the unhealthy odors that float on every breeze! Think, then, dear Friends, of the importance of being God's fragrant flowers which may yield perfumes that are delightful to Him—and that are blessed and healthful to our fellow men! A man of faith and love in a Church sweetens all his brethren. Give us but a few such in our midst and there shall be no broken spiritual unity! There shall be no coldness and spiritual death, but all shall go well where these men of God are among us as a mighty influence for good. And, as to the ungodly around us, the continued existence in the earth of the Church of Christ is the hope of the world! The world that hates the Church knows not what it does, for it is hating its best friend! The spices which God is conserving this present evil age, lest His anger should destroy it because of the growing corruption, are to be found in the flowers which He has planted in the garden of His Church!

It sometimes happens that *these sweet odors within God's people lie quiet and still*. There is a stillness in the air, something like that which the poet Coleridge makes "The Ancient Mariner" speak of in his graphic description of a calm within the tropics. Do you, dear Friends, ever get into that becalmed condition? I remember, when I was young, reading an expression—I think of Erskine's—in which he says that he likes a *roaring* devil better than a *sleeping* devil. It struck *me, then*, that if I could keep the devil always asleep, it would be the best thing that could possibly happen for me—but now I am not so sure I was right! At all events, I know this—when the old dog of Hell barks very loudly, he keeps me awake! And when he howls at me, he drives me to the Mercy Seat for protection. But when he goes to sleep and lies very quiet, I am very apt to go to sleep, too—and then the Graces that are within my soul seem to be absolutely hidden! And, mark you, hidden Grace, which in no way reveals itself by its blessed odors, is all the same as if there were none to those that watch from the outside and, sometimes, to the Believer himself!

What is needed, in order that he may know that he has these sweet perfumes, is something outside himself. You cannot stir your own Graces! You cannot make them more! You cannot cause their fragrance to flow forth! True, by prayer you may help to this end, but then that very prayer *is put into you by the Holy Spirit*—and when it has been offered to the Lord, it comes back to you laden with blessings. But often something more is needed—some movement of God's Providence and much more—some mighty working of His Grace to come and shake the flower bells in His garden and make them shed their fragrance in the air. Alas, on a hot and drowsy day, when everything has fallen into a deep slumber, even God's saints, though they are wise virgins, go as soundly asleep as the foolish virgins and they forget that "the Bridegroom comes!" "While the Bridegroom tarried, they all slumbered and slept" and, sometimes, you and I catch ourselves nodding when we ought to be wide awake! We are going through a part of that enchanted ground which John Bunyan describes and we do not know what to do to keep ourselves awake.

At such times, a Christian is very apt to ask, *"Am I, indeed, planted in God's garden? Am I really a child of God?"* Now I will say what some of you may think a strong thing, but I do not believe that he *is* a child of God who never raised that question! Cowper truly wrote—

> *"He has no hope who never had a fear.*
> *And he who never doubted of his state,*
> *He may, perhaps—perhaps he may—too late.*
> *I have sung and I expect that I may have to sing*
> *again—*
> *'Tis a point I long to know.*
> *Oft it causes anxious thought—*
> *Do I love the Lord or no?*
> *Am I His, or am I not?'"*

I cannot bear to get into that condition and I cannot bear to keep in it when I am in it, but still, there must be anxious thought about this all-important matter. Because you happened to be excited on a certain occasion and thought you were converted and were sure of Heaven, you had better look well to the evidence on which you are relying. You may be mistaken, after all, and while I would not preach up little faith, I would preach down great presumption! No man can have a faith too strong and no assurance can be too full if it really comes from God, the Holy Spirit. But if it comes merely out of your fancying that it is so and, therefore, will not examine yourself, whether you *are* in the faith, I begin to make up my mind that it is not so because you are afraid to look into the matter! "I know that I am getting rich," says a merchant. "I never keep any books and I do not need any books, but I know that I am getting on well in my business." If, my dear Sir, I do not soon see your name in the *Gazette*, I shall be rather surprised!

Whenever a man is so very good that he does not need to enquire at all into his position before God, I suspect that he is afraid of introspection and self-examination— and that he dare not look into his own heart! This I know, as I watch the many people of God committed to my care here—I see some run on for ten years or more serving God with holy joy and having no doubt or fear. They are not generally remarkable for any great depth of experience, but when God means to make mighty men of them, He digs about them and soon they come to me crying and craving a little comfort—telling me what doubts they have because they are not what they want to be! I am glad when this is the case, I rejoice because I know that they will be spiritually better off afterwards! They have reached a higher standard than they had previously attained. They have a better knowledge, now, of what they ought to be. It may be that, before, their ideal was a low one and they thought that they had reached it. But God has revealed to them greater heights which they have to climb—and they may as well gird up the loins of their mind to do so by Divine help!

As they get higher, they perhaps think, "Now we are at the top of the mountain," when they are really only on one of the lower spurs of it. Up they go, climbing again! "If once I reach that point, I shall soon be at the summit," you think. Yes, and when you have, at last, got there, you see the mountain still towering far above you! How deceptive is the height of the Alps to those who have not seen them before! I said to a friend, once, "It will take you about 13 hours to get to the top of that mountain." "Why," he replied, "I can run up in half-an-hour." I let him have a try and he had not gone far before he had to sit down to pant and rest. So you think of a certain height of Grace, "Oh, I can easily reach that!" Yes, just so, but you do not know how high it is. And those who think that they have reached the top do not know anything about the top, for he who knows how high is the holiness to which the Believer can attain will go on clambering and climbing, often on his hands and knees, and when he has reached that point which he *thought* was the summit, he will sit down and say, "I thought I had reached the top, but now I find that I have but begun the ascent." Or he may say with Job, "I have heard of You by the hearing of the ear," (and then I did not know much of You, or of myself, either), "but now my eye sees You. Therefore I abhor myself and repent in dust and ashes."

You see, then, that there are sweet spices lying in Christians, like hidden honey and locked-up perfume within the flowers on a hot day!

II. What is needed is that THOSE SWEET ODORS SHOULD BE DIFFUSED. That is to be our second head. Read the text again—"Awake, O north wind; and come, thou south; blow upon my garden, that the spices thereof may flow out."

Observe, first, that *until our Graces are diffused, it is the same as if they were not there.* You may go through a forest and it may be abounding in game, yet you may scarcely see a hare or notice a pheasant anywhere. There they lie, all quiet and undisturbed, but, by-and-by, the beaters go through the woods making a great noise and away the pheasants fly! And you may see the timid hares run like hinds let loose because they are disturbed and awakened. That is what we sometimes need, to be awakened and stirred from slumber! We may not know that we have any faith till there comes a trial—and then our faith starts boldly up! We can hardly know how much we love our Lord till there comes a test of our love—and then we so behave ourselves that we know that we *do* love Him. Oftentimes, as I have already reminded you, something is needed from without to stir the life that lies hidden within. It is so with these sweet flowers in the spouse's garden—they need either the north wind or the south wind to blow upon them that they may shed their sweet odors.

Notice next, that *it is very painful to a Christian to be in such a condition that his Graces are not stirring*. He cannot endure it! We who love the Lord were not born again to waste our time in sinful slumber! Our watchword is, "Let us not sleep, as do others." We were not born to inaction—every power that God has put within us was meant to be used in working, striving and serving the Lord! So, when our Graces are slumbering, we are in an unhappy state. Then we long for any agency that would set those Graces moving. The north wind? Oh, but if *it* shall blow, then we shall have snow! Well, then, let the snow come, for we must have our Graces set in motion—we cannot bear that they should continue to lie quiet and still. "Awake, O north wind!"— a heavy trial, a bleak adversity, a fierce temptation— *anything* so long as we do but begin to diffuse our

Graces! Or if the north wind is dreaded, we say, "Come, you south!" Let prosperity be granted to us! Let sweet fellowship with our Brothers and Sisters awaken us and holy mediations, full of delight, stir our souls! Let a sense of the Divine life, like a soft south wind, come to our spirit. We are not particular which it is, let the Lord send which He pleases, or both together, as the text seems to imply, only let us be awakened! "Quicken You me, O Lord, according to Your Word"—whichever Word you shall choose to apply—only quicken Your servant and let not the Graces within me be as if they were dead!

Remember, however, that *the best Quickener is always the Holy Spirit* and that blessed Spirit can come as the north wind, convincing us of sin and tearing away every rag of our self-confidence, or He may come as the soft south wind, all full of love, revealing Christ and the Covenant of Grace and all the blessings treasured for us therein. Come, Holy Spirit! Come as the Heavenly Dove, or as the rushing mighty wind, but come! Drop from above, as gently as the dew, or come like rattling hail, but come, blest Spirit of God! We feel that we must be moved, we must be stirred, and our heart's emotions must once again throb to prove that the life of God is really within us! And if we do not realize this quickening and stirring, we are utterly unhappy.

You see also, dear Friends, from this text, that *when a child of God sees that his Graces are not diffused abroad, then is the time that He should take to prayer*. Let no one of us ever think of saying, "I do not feel as if I could pray and, therefore, I will not pray." On the contrary, *then* is the time when you ought to pray more earnestly than ever! When the heart is disinclined for prayer, take that as a danger signal and, at once, go to the Lord with this resolve—

> *"I will approach You—I will force*
> *My way through obstacles to Thee!*
> *To You for strength will have recourse,*
> *To You for consolation flee!"*

When you seem to yourself to have little faith, and little love, and little joy, then cry to the Lord all the more! "Cry aloud and spare not." Say, "O my Father, I cannot endure this miserable existence! You have made me to be a flower, to shed abroad my perfume, yet I am not doing it. Oh, by some means stir my flagging spirit till I shall be full of earnest industry, full of holy anxiety to promote Your Glory, O my Lord and Master!" While you are thus crying, you must still believe, however, that God the Holy Spirit can stir your spirit and make you full of life again. Never permit a doubt about *that fact* to linger in your bosom, else you will be unnecessarily sad! You, who are the true children of God, can never come into a condition out of which the Holy Spirit cannot lift you up!

You remember the notable case of Laodicea, which was neither cold nor hot and, therefore, so nauseous to the great Lord that He threatened to spew her out of His mouth? Yet what is the message to the angel of that Church? "Behold, I stand at the door and knock." This is not said to *sinners*, it is addressed to the angel of the Church of the Laodiceans! "Behold, I stand at the door and knock: if any man hears my voice and opens the door, I will come in to him and will sup with him, and he with me." Oh, matchless Grace! He is sick of these lukewarm professors, yet He promises to sup with them and that they shall sup with Him! That is the only cure for lukewarmness and decline—to renew heart-fellowship with Christ—and He stands and offers it to all His people right now! "Only open the door, and I will sup with you, and you shall sup with Me."

O you whose Graces are lying so sinfully dormant, who have to mourn and cry because of "the body of this death"—for death in you seems to have taken to itself a body and to have become a substantial thing, no mere skeleton, but a heavy, cumbrous form that bows you down—cry to Him who is able to deliver you from this lukewarm and sinful state! Let every one of us put up the prayer of our text, "Awake, O north wind; and come, thou south; blow upon my garden, that the spices thereof may flow out."

III. Our third and closing head will help to explain the remaining portion of our text—"Let my Beloved come into His garden, and eat His pleasant fruits." These words speak of THE COMPANY OF CHRIST AND THE ACCEPTANCE OF OUR FRUIT BY CHRIST.

I want you, dear Friends, to especially notice one expression which is used here. While the spouse was, as it were, shut up and frozen, and the spices of the Lord's garden were not flowing out, she cried to the winds, "Blow upon *my* garden." She hardly dared to call it her Lord's garden! But now notice the alteration in the phraseology—"Let my Beloved come into *His* garden and eat His pleasant fruits." The wind has blown through the garden and made the sweet odors to flow forth—now it is no longer, "my garden," but, "His garden." It is wonderful how an increase of Grace transfers our properties! While we have but little Grace, we cry, "*my*," but when we get great Grace, we cry, "*His*." Wherein you are sinful and infirm, Brothers and Sisters, that is yours—you rightly call it "*my*"—but when you become strong and joyous, and full of faith, that is *not* yours! And you rightly call it, "*His*." Let Him have all the glory of the change while you take all the shame and confusion of face to yourself that ever you should have been so destitute of Grace! So the spouse says, "Let my Beloved come into His garden. Here are all the sweet perfumes flowing out. He will enjoy them—let Him come and feel Himself at home among them. He planted every flower and gave to each its fragrance—let Him come into His garden and see what wonders His Grace has worked."

Do you not feel, Beloved, that *the one thing you need to stir your whole soul is that Christ should come into it*? Have you lost His company lately? Oh, do not try to do without it! The true child of God ought not to be willing to bear broken communion for even five minutes, but should be sighing and crying for its renewal! Our business is to seek to "walk in the light as God is in the light," fully enjoying communion with Christ our Lord. But when that fellowship is broken, then the heart feels that it has cast all its happiness away and it must robe itself in sackcloth and sorrowfully fast. If the Presence of the Bridegroom shall be taken away from you, then, indeed, shall you have cause to fast and be sad. The best condition a heart can be in, if it has lost fellowship with Christ, is to resolve that it will give God no rest till it gets back to communion with Him—and to give *itself* no rest till once more it finds the Well-Beloved!

Next, observe that when the Beloved comes into His garden, the heart's humble but earnest entreaty is, "*Let Him eat His pleasant fruits*." Would you keep back anything from Christ? I know you could not if He were to come into His garden! The best things that you have, you would first present to Him, and then everything that you have, you would bring to Him and leave all at His dear feet. We do not ask Him to come to the garden that we may lay up our fruits, that we may put them by and store them up for *ourselves*—we ask Him to come and eat them. The greatest joy of a Christian is to give joy to

Christ! I do not know whether Heaven, itself, can exceed this pearl of giving joy to the heart of Jesus Christ on earth! It can match it, but not exceed it, for it is a superlative joy to give joy to Him—the Man of Sorrows, who was emptied of joy for our sakes and who now is filled up, again, with joy as each one of us shall come and bring his share and cause to the heart of Christ a new and fresh delight!

Did you ever reclaim a poor girl from the streets? Did you ever rescue a poor thief who had been in prison? Then I know that as you have heard of the holy chastity of the one, or of the sacred honesty of the other of those lives that you have been the means of restoring, you have said, "Oh, this is delightful! There is no joy equal to it! The effort cost me money, it cost me time, it cost me thought, it cost me prayer, but I am repaid a thousand times!" Then, as you see them growing up so bright, so transparent, so holy, so useful, you say, "This work is worth living for, it is a delight beyond measure!" Often persons come to me and tell me of souls that were saved through my ministry 20 years ago. I heard, the other day, of one who was brought to Christ by a sermon of mine nearly 30 years ago and I said to the friend who told me, "Thank you, thank you! You could not tell me anything that would give my heart such joy as this good news that God has made me the instrument of a soul's conversion." But what must be the joy of Christ who does all the work of salvation—who redeems us from sin, and death, and Hell—when He sees such creatures as we are made to be like Himself and knows the Divine possibilities of glory and immortality that lie within us?

What are we going to be, Brothers and Sisters, we who are in Christ? We have not any idea of what holiness, glory and bliss shall yet be ours! "It does not yet appear what we shall be." We may rise even while on earth to great heights of holiness—and the higher the better—but there is something better for us than mortal eyes have ever seen or mortal ears have ever heard! There is more Grace to be in the saints than we have ever seen in them, the saintliest saint on earth was never such a saint as they are, yonder, who are before the Throne of the Most High! And I know not but that, even when they get there, there shall be a something yet beyond for them and that through the eternal ages they shall still take for their motto, "Onward and upward!"

In Heaven, there will be no, "Finis." We shall still continue to develop and to become something more than we have ever been before—not fuller, but yet capable of holding more—always growing in the possibility of reflecting Christ and being filled with His love! And all the while our Lord Jesus Christ will be charmed and delighted with us. As He hears our lofty songs of praise, as He sees the bliss which will always be flashing from each one of us, as He perceives the Divine ecstasy which shall be ours forever, He will take supreme delight in it all! "My redeemed," He will say, "the sheep of My pasture, the purchase of My blood, borne on My shoulders, My very heart pierced for them, oh, how I delight to see them in the heavenly fold! These, My redeemed people, are joint heirs with Me in the boundless heritage that shall be theirs forever! Oh, how I delight in them!"

"Therefore, comfort one another with these words," Beloved, and cry mightily that, on this Church, and on all the Churches, God's Spirit may blow to make the spices flow! Pray, dear Friends, all of you, for the Churches to which you belong. And if you, my Brother, are a pastor, be asking especially for this Divine wind to blow through the garden which you have to cultivate, as I also pray for this portion of the garden of the Lord—"Let my Beloved come into His garden, and eat His pleasant fruits." The Lord be with each one of you, Beloved, for His dear name's sake! Amen.

A REFRESHING CANTICLE

DELIVERED ON A LORD'S DAY EVENING,
IN THE WINTER OF 1860,
BY C. H. SPURGEON

AT NEW PARK STREET CHAPEL, SOUTHWARK

"We will remember thy love more than wine."

Solomon's Song 1:4

THE Hebrew word for "love" here is in the plural—"We will remember Your loves." Think not, however, that the love of Jesus is divided, but know that it has different channels of manifestation. All the affections that Christ has, He bestows upon His Church and these are so varied that they may well be called "loves" rather than "love." The Septuagint translation is, "We will remember Your breasts." Bossuet, and many of the Romanist expositors who have brought much sanctity of thought and fervent appreciation of heart to bear upon this superlative Song, dilate very sweetly upon the word, "breasts," as it appears in the Latin Vulgate. I am disposed to be content with our own Version, with the alteration of one letter—"We will remember Your *loves* more than wine." By this expression we must understand, of course, all the love of Jesus, from the beginning even to the end, or, rather, to that eternity which has no end. We will remember those acts of love of which we have heard with our ears and our fathers have declared unto us. It has been told us by Inspired Prophets, and God has revealed it to us in His Word, by His Spirit, that Jesus Christ loved us from before the foundation of the world. We believe that His love is no passion of modern date—no mere spasm of pity. It is ancient as His Glory which He had with the Father before the world was—it is one of the things of eternity. This Divine Love is not a spring that welled up only a few days ago, but it is an everlasting fountain which has never ceased to flow!

We will remember, O Jesus, that love of Yours which was displayed in the council chamber of eternity, when You did, on our behalf, interpose as the Daysman and Mediator—when You did strike hands with Your Father and become our Surety and take us as Your betrothed! We will remember that love which moved You to undertake a work so burdensome to accomplish, an enterprise which none but Yourself could ever have achieved! We will remember the love which suggested the Sacrifice of Yourself. The love which, until the fullness of time, mused over that Sacrifice and longed for the hour of which, in the volume of the Book it was written of You, "Lo, I come." We will remember Your love, O Jesus, as it was manifested to us in Your holy life, from the manger of Bethlehem to the garden of Gethsemane! We will track You from the cradle to the grave, for every word and every deed of Yours was love. You, wherever You did walk, did scatter lovingkindness

109

with both Your hands. As it is said of Your Father, "God is Love," so, surely, You are Love, O Jesus! The fullness of the Godhead dwells in You! The essence of love, nothing else but love, is Your Incarnate Person.

And especially, O Jesus, will we remember Your love to us upon the Cross! We will view You as You come from the garden of Your agony and from the hall of Your flagellation. We will gaze upon You with Your hands and Your feet nailed to the accursed tree. We will watch You when You could, if You had willed it, have saved Yourself, but when You did, nevertheless, give up Your strength and bow Yourself downward to the grave that You might lift us up to Heaven. We will remember Your love which You did manifest through Your poor, bleeding hands and feet and side. We will remember this love of Yours till it invigorates and cheers us "more than wine"—the love of which we have heard, which You have exercised since Your death—the love of Your Resurrection, the love which prompts You to continually intercede before Your Father's Throne, that burning lamp of Love which will never let you hold Your peace until Your chosen ones are all safely housed, Zion is glorified and the spiritual Jerusalem is settled on her everlasting foundations of light and love in Heaven! We will remember all Your love, from its beginning in the eternal past to the eternity that is to come—no, we will try to project our thoughts and imagination—and so to remember that as long as eternity shall continue, even forever and forevermore, so long shall Your love exists in all its Glory, undiminished in its luster or its force! "We will remember Your love more than wine."

Nor is this all the love we have to remember. Though we ought to recollect what we have heard and what we have been taught, I think the spouse means more than this, "We will remember Your loves"—not only what we have been told, but what we have *felt*. Come, dear Hearers, let each one of you speak for yourselves, or, rather, you think of this for yourselves and let me speak of it for you. I will remember Your love, O Jesus—Your love to me when I was a stranger, wandering far from God. The love which restrained me from committing deadly sin and withheld my hands from self-destruction! I will remember the love which tracked me in my course—

"When Satan's blind slave, I sported with death."

I will remember the love which held back the axe when Justice said, "Cut it down; why cumbers it the ground?" I will remember the love that took me into the wilderness and stripped me, there, of all my self-righteousness—and made me feel my weight of guilt and the burden of my iniquity. Especially will I remember the love which said to me, "Come unto Me, and I will give you rest." I cannot forget that matchless love which, in a moment, washed my sins away and made my spotted soul white as the driven snow! Can you forget, my Brothers and

Sisters, that happiest of days when Jesus first whispered to you, "I am yours and you are Mine"? I can never forget the transporting hour when He spoke thus to me! It is as fresh in my memory right now as if it had only happened this afternoon! I could sing of it if it were right to stop a sermon for a sonnet—I could sing of that love, passing all measure, which took my soul and washed it in the precious blood of Jesus and then clothed it in the spotless robe of His righteousness! O Love Divine, You excel all other loves, that You could deal with such a rebellious, traitorous worm and make that worm an heir of Heaven!

But we have more love than this to remember—all the love that we have felt since then. I will remember the valley of Baca and the Hill Mizar. Nor shall my soul forget those chambers of fellowship where You have unveiled Yourself to me. If Moses had his cleft in the rock where he could see the back parts of his God, we also have had our clefts in the rock where we have seen the full splendors of the Godhead in the Person of Christ! Did David remember the tracks of the wild goat where he was hunted on the mountains—the cave of Adullam, the land of Jordan and of the Hermonites? We, too, can remember spots equally dear to these in blessedness. "The Lord has appeared of old unto me, saying, Yes, I have loved you with an everlasting love: therefore with lovingkindness I have drawn you." Christian, can you not recollect the sweet exchanges there have been between yourself and your Lord when you have left your griefs at His feet and left with a song? Can you not remember some happy seasons when you went to Him empty, and came away full? Is your heart heavy just now? It has not always been so. There have been times when, like David, you could dance before the Lord! Times of holy merriment when, like Miriam, you could strike your timbrel and say to those around you, "Sing to the Lord, for He has triumphed gloriously." There have been times when Jesus and you have not been strangers to one another, for He has linked His arms in yours and walked along with you! And there have been other times when your head has been upon His bosom and you could feel His heart beating with warm love to you.

Thus, then, in the summary of Christ's loves, which I will now humbly endeavor to pass in review, it will be necessary for me to mention not only the love we have heard about, but the love we have felt and enjoyed. Do not suppose, dear Brothers and Sisters, that I am able to refresh your memories upon this sacred subject. It is the Holy Spirit's work to assist you in that matter! But I do trust that the resolution contained in our text will be formed in the heart of every one of you—"We will remember Your loves more than wine"—and that you will have the Grace to carry out that resolution.

I. Here then, Beloved, we have a RESOLUTION POSITIVELY EXPRESSED—"We *will* remember Your love."

Why does the spouse speak so positively? Because she is Inspired—she is not like Simon Peter when he said, "Although all shall be offended, yet will not I." She is speaking the Truth of God, for she will not forget the love of her Lord. Why is that? For one very good reason—because she cannot. If the Church could forget Christ's love to her, she would do so. She is such a forgetful wife that all her Husband's affections would be lost upon her, were it possible. But that cannot be— there is something about the love of Christ that makes it adhere to those upon whom it is bestowed—we cannot forget it. It enters into the heart like wine that seasons the cask, and the scent thereof abides. It pervades the soul. It permeates every faculty. It brings the secret thoughts into obedience to Christ. It flows through every vein of hope and fear, passion and desire. So the spouse could truthfully say to her Lord, "We will remember Your love." The virtue was not in her own constancy, but in the tenacity of His affection—therefore she could not help remembering it!

What is there, in the love of Christ, that will compel us to remember it? The things that we recollect best are of certain kinds.

Some that we remember best have been *sublime things*. When we have stood, for the first time, where we could see a lofty mountain whose snowy summit pierced the thick ebon clouds, we have said, "We shall never forget this sight." When Humboldt, the great traveler, had his first view of the vast prairies of North America, he declared that he could never forget the sensations of that moment. I can imagine how Dr. Livingstone, when he first came in sight of the magnificent falls which he discovered, might well say, "To my dying day, I shall hear the rushing of that tremendous stream of water." I can myself remember an unusually violent thunderstorm, when the lightning flew across the heavens, flash after flash, without a moment's pause, as though a thousand suns were dashing through the sky. I recollect the consternation of men and women when a neighboring house was struck by the lightning and burnt with a terrific blaze which could scarcely be seen by reason of the brightness of the lightning. My recollection of that terrible scene will never depart from me! The sublimity of what we have seen often causes us to remember it. So is it with the love of Christ. How it towers to Heaven! And mark how brightness succeeds brightness, how flash follows after flash of unspeakable love and full of glory! There is no pause, no interval of darkness, no chasm of forgetfulness. Its sublimity compels us to remember its manifestation.

Again, we are pretty sure to remember *unusual things*. If we were asked whether we remembered that the sun had risen, we might say, "It is not a matter of memory at all. I feel certain that it did, though I did not see it." But if we are asked if we ever saw an eclipse, "Oh, yes!" we reply, "we recollect that! We remember watching it and how disappointed we were because it was not as dark as we expected it to be." Many people do not notice the stars much, but who forgets a comet? Everybody recollects the phenomenon of nature because it is unusual. When we see something strange, uncommon, out of the ordinary, the memory at once fixes upon it and holds it fast. So is it with the love of Christ. It is such an extraordinary thing, such a marvelous thing that the like was never known! Ransack history and you cannot find its parallel. There is but one love that is like it—that is the love of the Father to His only-begotten Son. Besides this, there is nothing to which we can compare the love of Christ to His people. That constellation of the Cross is the most marvelous that is to be seen in the spiritual sky! The eyes, once spellbound by its charms, must retain undying admiration because it is the greatest wonder of wonders and miracle of miracles which the universe ever saw!

Sometimes, too, things which are not important in themselves are fixed on the memory because of *certain circumstances* which happen in association with them. The country people often say, if you ask them whether they recollect such-and-such a year, "Ah, Master! It was the year of the hard frost, wasn't it?" Another time they will say, "Why, yes! That was the year when the blight fell upon our gardens and all our potatoes were of no use—and we were nearly starved that winter." Circumstances help to make us remember facts. If something particular in politics should happen on our birthday, or our wedding day, or on some other notable occasion, we would say, "Oh, yes! I remember that—it happened the day I was married, or the day So-and-So was buried." Now, we can never forget the love of Christ because the circumstances were so peculiar when, for the first time, we knew anything at all about it! We were plunged in sin and ruin! We were adrift on the great sea of sin! We had no hope, we were ready to sink and no shore was near—but Jesus came and saved us! We can never forget those circumstances—with some of us, they were truly awful, beyond all description. Therefore we cannot forget the time when Jesus' love first dawned upon our minds.

I think, my dear Friends, I might give you 20 reasons why it would be impossible for the children of God to forget the love of Christ to them, but above and beyond every other reason is this one, *Christ will not let His people forget His love*. If, at any time, He finds them forgetful, He will come to them and refresh their memories. If all the love they have ever enjoyed should be forgotten by them, He will give them some fresh manifestations of love. "Have you forgotten My Cross?" He asks, "then I will cause you to remember it afresh, for at My Table I will manifest Myself to you as I have not done of late. Do you forget what I did for you in the council chamber of eternity? Then I will remind you of it, for you still need a Counselor and I will come to your relief just when you are at your wits' end—and I will give you wisdom. Have you forgotten that I called you to Myself when you were a stranger? I will bring you back from your wanderings and then you will remember Me again." Mothers do not let their children forget them if they can help it. If the boy has gone to Australia and he does not write home, his mother writes to him, "Has my John forgotten his mother?" Then there comes back a sweet epistle which lets the mother know that the gentle hint she gave him was not lost. So is it with Christ—He often says to one of His forgetful children, "What? Is your heart cold to Him who loved you so much that He could not live in Heaven without you, but must come to earth, go out into the wilderness, up to the Cross and down to the grave in order to find you?" You can be sure that He will have our hearts! Prone to wander, He knows that they are, and we feel it ourselves, but He will have them. Oh, that He would drive the nail of the Cross right through your heart, that it might be forever fastened there! Painful might the process be—some sharp affliction might tear your flesh—yet, if that would bring you near your Lord and keep you near Him, you might thank Him even for the affliction and love Him all the more because of it!

II. Now let us advance another step and look at THE COMPARATIVE RESOLUTION—"We will remember Your love *more than wine*."

Why is "wine" mentioned here? I take it to be used here as a figure. The fruit of the vine represents the chief of earthly luxuries. "I will remember Your love more than the choicest or most exhilarating comforts which this world can give me." We have many things which we might compare to wine, in the good and in the bad sense, too—good, because they cheer, comfort and invigorate—bad, because when we rely upon them, they intoxicate, they overthrow and cast down to the ground. We very readily remember the good things of earth for a season. When creature comforts abound with us and we have happy and merry days, we remember them. And when nights of darkness come upon us, we remember the days of our brightness and we talk of them. It is so with the widow bereaved of her husband—she remembers the days of her happiness, when the partner of her joy was with her. She recollects his affectionate words and his sweet deeds of love. In the case of the mother bereaved of her child, she recalls the love that child had to her and the solace it was to her when her little one slept on her bosom. Have you become poor? Then the "wine" that you remember is the wealth you once possessed—you remember how you had no need to tramp over weary miles and to shiver in the wintry cold. Now that your pain has come, you remember your former joy and it makes your present pain all the more painful. This, "wine," may be to a minister, the joy of being successful—and there may come to him days when his chapel will be half-empty and then he will look back, with regret, upon the joys he once possessed. The spouse says, "We will remember Your love more than all earthly comforts." She cannot help doing so. If she could, she would remember the *world* rather than Heaven! She would have a remembrance of creature comforts and she would be forgetful of her Lord.

The fact is, the impression which the love of Christ makes on the true Believer is far *greater and deeper* than the impression which is made by anything earthly. Mere mortal joys write their record on the sand and their memory is soon erased, but Christ's love is like an inscription cut deeply into marble—the remembrance of it is deeply engraved in our hearts. The joy of the creature is something like a lithograph cut lightly on the stone—when the stone is cleaned, the picture is gone. But the love of Christ is like the steel engraving—it is deeply cut and cannot be easily erased. Earthly joys tread with light feet and leave but a faint impression— but the love of Christ treads into the very core of our soul at every footstep and, therefore it is that we remember it better than we remember any earthly pleasure!

Earthly comforts, too, like wine, leave but a *mingled impression*. In the cup of joy there is a dash of sorrow. There is nothing we have here below which is not somewhat tainted with grief. Solomon has warned us against the sparkling wine—"Look not upon the wine when it is red, when it gives his color in the cup, when it moves itself aright. At the last it bites like a serpent, and stings like an adder." Even friendship, the very cream of joy, trembles on the confines of disappointment, as it is written, "Cursed be the man that trusts in man, and makes flesh his arm." But in Christ's love there is nothing for you to ever regret. When you have enjoyed it to the fullest, you cannot say that there has been any bitterness in it. When you have come forth from the secret chamber of communion with your Lord, you have realized the purity of His love—there has been nothing to qualify your enjoyment of it. When you have been to a party of your friends, you have said, "I have been very happy, *but*—I could not enjoy myself there six days in a week." But when you have been with Christ, you have felt that you could enjoy yourself in that way to all eternity! You could not have too much of such fellowship, for there was nothing in it to mar your happiness. True, there is the remembrance of your sin, but that is so sweetly covered by your Lord's forgiveness and graciousness that His love is, indeed, better than wine! It has had all the good effects of wine, but none of its ill results.

Equally true is it that the remembrance of earth's comforts, of which wine is the type, must be but *transient*. If the sinner could live many days and have much wealth, would he remember it when he entered the unseen world? Ah, he might remember it, but it would be with awful sighs and sobs! You know how Abraham spoke, across the great gulf, to the rich man in Hell, "Son, remember that you in your lifetime received your good things, and likewise Lazarus evil things: but now he is comforted and you are tormented." But we can say of the love of Christ, that it is better than wine, for we shall rejoice to remember it in eternity—

> *"There, on a green and flowery mount,*
> *Our weary souls shall sit*
> *And with transporting joys recount."*

What shall we recount? Dr. Watts says—

> *"The labors of our feet,"*

but I do not think so. I believe we shall recount the labors of Him who lived and died for us! That is what we shall talk of in Heaven—I am sure that this is the theme of all the music and songs of Paradise—

> *"Jesus, the Lord, their harps employ,*
> *Jesus, my Love, they sing!*
> *Jesus, the life of all our joy*
> *Sounds sweet from every string."*

Do you not see, then, why this comparison is made in our text? We remember Christ's love more than the best earthly comforts because they make but a feeble impression, a mingled impression, a marred impression, and their impression, at best, is but transient. But the love of Christ is remembered as something that is better than wine. I have to hurry over these different points, but if you enjoy hearing about this subject as much as I delight in preaching upon it, you would not mind listening to me all night long! And I should not mind preaching right through the night. Surely, this is a theme that sets one's tongue at a happy liberty. "My tongue is the pen of a ready writer" if I can but feel the love of Christ shed abroad in my heart!

III. Now, thirdly, I am to speak of THE PRACTICAL EFFECTS OF REMEMBERING CHRIST'S LOVE.

If we remember the love of Christ to us, the first practical effect will be that *we shall love Him*. Can I remember Your love to me, O my sweet Lord, and not love You in return? Surely, Dr. Watts was right when he wrote—

> *"Come, Holy Spirit, heavenly Dove,*
> *With all Your quickening powers!*
> *Come, shed abroad a Savior's love,*
> *And that shall kindle ours."*

True it is, O Jesus, that there is no light of love in our hearts except the light of Your love! It is the holy fire from Your altar that must kindle the incense in the censer of our hearts. There is no living water to be drawn out of these dry wells! You, O Jesus, must supply them from the bubbling spring in Your own heart! When my heart is conscious of Your love, it loves You in return.

Another practical effect of remembering Christ's love will be *love to the brethren*. When we remember Christ's love as we ought, we shall not meet one of Christ's brethren without falling in love with him directly. Christ has some very poor brethren and some very unhandsome ones. David sent to enquire whether there were any left of the house of Saul to whom he might show kindness for Jonathan's sake. Ziba told him that Jonathan had a son named Mephibosheth who was lame in his feet. What did David do when he heard this? Did he say, "I will have nothing to do with him—I do not want a lame fellow stumbling about my place"? Oh, no—he might be lame in his feet, but he was Jonathan's son—so David sent for him and said to him, "You shall eat bread at my table continually." Did you ever know one of Christ's beloved who was lame in his feet? There is a little lameness, somewhere or other, about all of them—and if we only love those saints who are very holy, it will seem as if we only loved them for their own sakes. But if we love Christ's deformed and crippled children, that looks like loving them for His sake! And, I think, if you could remember what a clumsy child you were, yourself, you would not look with such disdain upon any of God's other children!

Ministers have much to bear in connection with some of their people. One man's judgment is so keen that you are always afraid of saying something amiss in his presence. Another man's temper is so hot that you cannot meddle with him for fear you should provoke a quarrel. Another man is so worldly that although he has the Grace of God in his heart, it seems to be only like a spark in damp tinder. Christ has many very unseemly children—yet if we can but see that they are Christ's—if they have only a little likeness to Him, we love them directly for His sake and are willing to do what we can for them out of love to Him! The remembrance of the love of Christ to us will, I repeat, always kindle in us a love towards all the brethren!

The next effect will be *holy practice*. When we remember the love of Christ to us, we shall hate sin. Feeling that He has bought us with His precious blood, we shall abhor the very name of iniquity. When Satan tempts us, we shall, each one say, "Get you gone, for I will have nothing to do with you—I remember Christ's love to me." Have you ever heard the story of the Indian woman who, when she was enticed by some great chief who wished to lead her astray, made to him this noble answer, "I know no one in the world to be beautiful or attractive but my husband"? So will the Believer say, when he is tempted, "I know of nothing that is good but Christ. I know of no one who is so fair as He is. So be gone, black Satan—my heart is given wholly to Christ and I will have nothing to do with you."

Another effect of remembering the love of Christ will be *repose of heart in time of trouble*. When we have, for a while lost the light of God's Countenance. When we are like the Apostle in that great storm at sea and are in a place where two seas meet and our vessel is already broken by the violence of the waves. When darkness increases our fears, or daylight reveals fresh dangers, then is it especially sweet to remember the love of our

Lord! In such a time as that, the tried Believer can say, "He did love me once and His love never changes. Though I cannot now see the light of His Countenance, I know that He is still the same as He always was. I remember the garden of delights where He revealed His love to me and the banqueting house where He gave me such choice fare—and I feel persuaded that He has not forgotten His poor spouse, but that He will come to her, again, and once more lift her out of the mire, set her feet upon a rock, put a new song into her mouth and establish her goings."

A constant remembrance of Christ's love to us will make us always cheerful, dutiful, and holy! Dear Lord, grant us this gift, for if You will enable us to remember Your love more than wine, You will give us all good things in one! Let Your good Spirit but keep us up to this good resolution and we shall be both holy and happy, honoring You and rejoicing in You!

IV. Lastly, I would put before you A FEW PRACTICAL SUGGESTIONS AS TO PRESERVING A DEEPER AND MORE SINCERE REMEMBRANCE OF CHRIST'S LOVE.

The old Puritan divines frequently compared their hearers to the Egyptian dog that ran to the Nile and drank and then ran away. They came up to the meeting house and heard the minister, took a little sip of the Gospel, which sufficed them, and then they were off! One preacher said that he wished they were like the fishes—not come and lap at the stream, as the dog did, but swim in it and live in it! There are too many, in this age, who are content with hearing a little of Christ's love—a sip by the way is all that they seem to need. But it would be far better if you could come up to Rutherford's ideal—"I would have my soul sunk over its masthead in a sea of love to Christ. I would be sunk 50 fathoms deep in the mighty shoreless ocean of His love so that there might be nothing left of me, and that I might be swallowed up in love to Christ—and in Christ's love to me."

I expect, dear Brothers and Sisters, that your complaint is that you cannot remember good things as you would. I know very well how you feel. You hear a sermon and become, for a while, absorbed in holy meditation—but you have to return to your shop early tomorrow morning and you only left it as late as twelve o'clock on Saturday night. There are six days for the world and only one for Heaven! It is no wonder that you find the sermon so difficult to remember. You remind me of a person going out into a garden on a dark night, carrying a lighted candle. If the wind should blow, there is such a careful shielding of the light with the hand, lest it should be blown out. In like manner, it is but a feeble light that you bear away from the public ministry and there are ten thousand winds blowing around you trying to put it out! You must, indeed, be careful to keep it alight all the week in your memory. Let me give you a little practical advice as to how you may keep constantly in your mind a remembrance of Jesus Christ's love.

One of the first things I would recommend to you is *frequent meditation*. See if you cannot more often get a quarter of an hour all alone, that you may sit down and turn over and over again the love of Christ to you. Remember that souls grow more by meditation than by anything else. The cattle go round the fields and eat the grass—that is like hearing the Word. But, afterwards, they lie down in a quiet corner and chew the cud—that is like meditation upon what we have heard. Get a quarter of an hour, if you can, to masticate and digest the Word of God. "A quarter of an hour!" says someone, "why, I could not get five minutes!" I would not be hard with you, dear Brother, but I think you could. Days can sometimes be pulled out either at one end or at the other. If you cannot lengthen the day at the night end, cannot you pull it out at the morning end? Is there not a possibility of a little saving of time at some hour during the day? You will do none the less work for allowing time for meditation and prayer. Our old proverb says, "Prayer and provender hinder no man's journey," and I believe that prayer and meditation hinder no man's work! Try to get a little time to think about your soul. What? So much time to be occupied with this dusty, sinful world, and so little time to be devoted to that which relates to Heaven? So much time to be employed concerning meat, drink and clothes, and so little time to be given to thoughts of our precious Savior and all His loveliness? Get a little time alone, Beloved, for that will help to keep you right. You would not forget your Master's love nearly as much as you do if you would secure more time for meditation upon it.

Another means of remembering Christ's love is this. *Take care that you are not content with what you knew of Christ's love yesterday.* You need to know a little more about it today and you ought to know still more about it tomorrow. Some Christians do not commune with their Lord nearly as often as they ought. I wonder how they manage to live on in such a fashion. They get a little manna once a month and they try to live on that until another month comes round. They meet with their Savior, perhaps, at the Communion Table—and not always then—and they are content to live from day to day without having fellowship with Him. Be not you one of that order of Christians! Seek for daily—no, more than that—*constant* communion with the Lord Jesus Christ! You are to pray for daily bread—then, surely, He who bade you do that must mean that you should seek to be fed daily with Himself, who is the Bread of Heaven! I do not like to hear people talk about what they knew of Jesus five of six years ago unless they can also tell something of what they know of Him now! What would you think of a wife who said, "My husband spoke kindly to me some years ago and I saw him five years ago, but I have not seen him since"? You would say, "How can the woman live, if she is a loving wife, without seeing her husband? Is he in the same house with her and yet has he not spoken to her all that while?

The Lord Jesus is always near to you and do you mean to say that you can live without fellowship with Him? Yes, you can, for some of you do! But I pray you not to live so any longer, for it is a poor, starving way of dragging on a miserable existence! You have just enough religion to make you wretched! You have not enough to make you happy—get a great deal more of it! Drink deeply at the heavenly spring of fellowship. If you learn a little more about Christ every day, you will not be likely to forget what you already know of Him.

Then, again, as another way of keeping in your heart what you do know—*take care, when you have a sense of Christ's love, that you let it go down deeply.* If there were a nail so placed that it would slacken its hold a little every day for six days—if I had the opportunity of driving it in the first day—I would try to drive it in right up to the head and to clinch it. So, if you have not much time for fellowship and communion with Christ—if you have only a short season for meditation, try to drive the nail well home. Do not be content with merely *thinking* about Christ—seek to *see* Him before your eyes as manifestly crucified. See Him as He groans in the Garden and do not be content unless you can groan with Him. See Him as He hangs upon the Cross and do not rest satisfied until you can feel that you are crucified with

Him. Realize your fellowship with Him as He rises from the tomb, for this will help very much to keep you right.

I have heard the story of a man who was passing by a house where a poor idiot lad, with a piece of sandpaper, was souring away at a brass plate. The man asked what he was doing and he replied, "I am trying to scour the name out." "Ah," said the other, "You may scour away as long as you like, but you will never be able to do that." And so, I think I see the Devil scouring away at some of you, trying to get the name of Jesus out of your heart. Scour away, Satan, if you like, but you will never get it out, for it is too deeply cut! If Christ's name is engraved upon your heart, Satan may try to get it out, but he will never succeed in doing so! It shall never be obliterated, but shall shine all the more brightly for his attempts to remove it!

Let me add one more direction. When any of you meet together, it is always a good thing to *make Christ the theme of your conversation*. Oh, what a deal of idle gossip there is, even on Sundays! Many people do not go out on Sunday afternoon, so they must talk about something. They do not like to talk about their trade— they fancy that would be too secular. They do not like to talk about strictly sacred things—they think that might appear hypocritical. So they begin, "Have you ever heard So-and-So preach?" "Yes, I did once." "Did you like him?" So, from one, they go on to others—and ministers and their sermons become the bones that they pick on

Sunday afternoons! They feel that they must have some theme for their conversation not quite sacred, nor wholly secular. I would advise you to talk more about the Lord Jesus Christ than you have been—you will be less likely to forget His love if you are often talking of Him. Let the music of His name ring in your ears all the day long—and if you would have it ring in your ears, it must ring from your tongue! Whenever you have the opportunity, tell out the marvelous story of His great love to you and so will your own memory be refreshed and others, listening to your testimony, will also get a large and, it may be, an everlasting blessing!

May God now grant to you, my dear Hearers, that you may retain a sense of Christ's love to you if you have ever enjoyed it! If you never have, may God now give it to you! If you have never come to Christ, come to Him now! Remember that Jesus loves sinners. Those who are now farthest from Him, when they once return to Him, shall know that He loves them. If you, "take with you words," and come to Him, groaning and sighing, He will not cast you out. He stands now with open arms and freely invites you! Come to Him, I beseech you. As His ambassador, I entreat you to come. If you do so, He will fold you to His bosom. All that the heirs of Heaven can have, you shall have! All that the glorified saints are now enjoying shall yet be your privilege, also! You shall one day walk with Christ in white, and see His face, and be with Him in Paradise and be blessed throughout eternity! May God grant us His Grace that our text may become the cheerful sonnet of our experience—"We will remember Your love more than wine."

PRAY THAT THE HOLY SPIRIT WILL USE THIS SERMON TO BRING MANY TO A SAVING KNOWLEDGE OF JESUS CHRIST.

THE BEST OF THE BEST

DELIVERED ON THURSDAY EVENING,
MAY 19TH, 1881
BY C. H. SPURGEON

AT THE METROPOLITAN TABERNACLE, NEWINGTON.

"I am the rose of Sharon, and the lily of the valleys."
Song of Solomon 2:1

THE time of flowers has come and as they are in some faint degree, emblems of our Lord, it is well, when God thus calls, that we should seek to learn what He desires to teach us by them. If nature now spreads out her roses and her lilies, or prepares to do so, let us try not only to see them, but to see Christ as He is shadowed forth in them. "I am the rose of Sharon, and the lily of the valleys." If these are the words of the Well-Beloved—and I have no doubt that they are—then it may be suggested by some that here we have the Savior praising Himself—and it is true—but in no unworthy sense, for well may He praise Himself since no one else can do it as it should be done! There is no human language that can ever set forth His beauties as they deserve to be told. As good John Berridge says—

> *"Living tongues are dumb at best,*
> *We must die to speak of Christ"*

as He should be spoken of. He will never fully be described unless He shall describe Himself. For certain, we should never have known God if He had not revealed

Himself—and every good thing that you or I know of Him, He, Himself, has told us. We make no discoveries of God except as God discovers Himself to us. If, then, any quibblers were to find fault with the Christ of God because He commends Himself, I would answer, Does not God commend Himself and must not His well-beloved Son do the same? Who else is there that can possibly reveal Him to us unless He unveils His own face to our admiring gaze?

Moreover, let it always be remembered that human self-praise is evil because of the motive which underlies it. When we praise ourselves—and, alas, that we should be so foolish as to do so—we do it out of pride! But when Christ praises Himself, He does it out of *humility*. "Oh," you say, "how can you *prove* that to be true?" Why, thus—He praises Himself that He may win our love—but what *condescension* it is on His part that He should care about the love of such insignificant and undeserving persons as we are! It is a wonderful stoop that the Christ of God should speak about having a *bride* and that He should come to seek His bride among the sons of men! If princes were to look for consorts among beggars, that would be, after all, but a small stoop, for God has made of one blood all nations of men that dwell upon the face of the earth. But for Christ to forsake the thrones and glories of Heaven, and the splendors of His Father's courts above to come down to win a well-beloved one here and, for her sake, to take upon Himself her nature—and in her nature to bear the shame of death, even the death of the Cross—this is stupendous condescension of which only God, Himself, is capable! And this praising of Himself is a part of that condescension—a necessary means of winning the love of the heart that He has chosen.

So this is a matchless instance, not of pride, but of *humility*, that those dear lips of the heavenly Bridegroom should have to speak to His own commendation and that He should say, "I am the rose of Sharon, and the lily of the valleys." O human lips, why are you silent, so that Christ must speak about Himself? O human hearts, why are you so hard that you will never feel until Christ, Himself, shall address you? O human eyes, why are you so blind that you shall never see till Christ shows Himself in His own superlative light and loveliness? I think I need not defend my Master, though He used these sweet emblems to set forth Himself, for this is an instance, not of His pride, but of His humility.

It is also an instance of the Master's wisdom, for as it is His design to win hearts to Himself, He uses the best means of winning them. How are hearts won? Very often by the exhibition of beauty. Love at first sight has been begotten by the vision of a lovely countenance. Men and women, too, are struck with affection through the eyes when they perceive some beauty which charms and pleases them. So the Savior lifts the corner of the veil that conceals His glories and lets us see some glimpse of His beauty in order that He may win our hearts. There are some who seem to think that they can bully men to Christ, but that is a great mistake. It is very seldom that sinners can be driven to the Savior—His way is to *draw* them. He Himself said, "I, if I am lifted up from the earth, will draw all men to Me. This He said, signifying what death He should die." And the drawings of Christ are not, as it were, with a cart rope, but with silken bonds, yes, with invisible chains, for His beauty is of such a character that it creates love! His beauty is so attractive that it draws the heart! So, in infinite wisdom, our Lord Jesus Christ sets forth His own beauties that He may, thereby, win our hearts.

I believe that there is no preaching like the exaltation of Christ Crucified. There is nothing so likely to win the sons of men as a sight of Him and if God the Holy Spirit will but help all His ministers, and help all His people to set forth the beauties of Christ, I shall not doubt that the same Spirit will incline men's hearts to love Him and to trust Him! Note, then, the condescension and also the wisdom which are perceptible in this self-commendation on the part of Christ—"I am the rose of Sharon, and the lily of the valleys."

I think that our Lord also speaks thus as an encouragement to timid souls. His tender familiarity in praising Himself to us is one of the most effectual proofs of His lowliness. Does Christ commend Himself to us? Does He say to us, for instance, "I am meek and lowly in heart"? What is His objective in speaking thus but that we may take His yoke upon us and may learn of Him and find rest to our souls? And if He says, "I am the rose of Sharon," what does He mean but that we may pluck Him and take Him for our own? If He says, "I am the lily of the valleys," why does He take the trouble to tell us that but because He wants us to *take* Him and to *have* Him for our very own? I think that it is so sweet of Christ to praise Himself in order to show that He longs for us to come to Him! He declares Himself to be a fountain of living water, but why is He a fountain but that we may come to Him and drink? He tells us, "I am the bread which came down from Heaven," but why does He speak of Himself as bread, except that if a man eats, he shall never hunger? Why, because He wants us to partake of Him! You need not, therefore, be afraid that He will refuse you when you come to Him. If a man praises his wares, it is that he may sell them. If a doctor advertises his cures, it is that sick folk may be induced to try his medicine. And when our Lord Jesus Christ praises Himself, it is a kind of holy advertisement by which He would tempt us to "come, buy wine and milk without money and without price." If He praises Himself, it is that we may fall in love with Him—and we need not be afraid to come and lay our poor hearts at His feet and ask Him to accept us—for He would not have wooed us by unveiling His beauties if He had meant, after all, to trample on our hearts, and say, "I care nothing for such poor love as yours."

I feel most grateful, then, that I have not, at this time, so much to praise my Master as to let Him speak His own praises, for, "never man spoke like this Man!" When He commends Himself, what would have been folly in others is wisdom in Him! And whereas we say to our fellow man, "Let another man praise you, and not your own mouth," I would say to Christ, "My Master, praise Yourself, for You alone can do it as it ought to be done! As for Your poor servant, he would try to be an echo of Your voice, and that will be infinitely better than anything he, himself, can say."

I think, also, that there is good reason for our Lord to praise Himself in the fashion that He does in our text because, after all, it is not praise. "What?" you ask, "and yet you have been talking all this while as if it *were* praise." Well, so it is in one sense, to us, but it is not to Christ. Suppose the sun were to compare itself with a glowworm—would that be praise? Suppose an angel were to compare himself with an ant, would that be praise? And when my Lord and Master, whose eyes outshine the sun, and who is infinitely higher than the mightiest of the angels, compares Himself to a rose and a lily, is that praise? Well, it is to you and to me, but it certainly cannot be to Him! It is a marvelous stoop for Christ, who is "God over all, blessed forever," and the Light of the universe, to say, "I am a rose; I am a lily." O my blessed Lord, this is a sort of Incarnation, as when the Eternal God did take upon Himself an infant's form!

So here, the Everlasting God says, "I am"—and what comes next?—"a rose and a lily." It is an amazing stoop! I know not how to set it forth to you by human language—it is a sort of verbal rehearsal of what He did afterwards when, though He counted it not robbery to be equal with God, "He took upon Himself the form of a Servant, and was made in the likeness of sinful flesh, and became obedient to death, even the death of the Cross." "I am God, yet," He says, "I am the rose of Sharon, and the lily of the valleys."

What does our text mean? I think it means that our Lord Jesus Christ is exceedingly delightful, so, let us speak, first, of *the exceeding delightfulness of our Lord*. And then, inasmuch as He uses *two* emblems—first the rose, and then the lily—surely this is to express *the sweet variety of His delightfulness*. And, inasmuch as He speaks of Himself as the rose of Sharon, and the lily of the valleys, I shall have to show you, in the last place, that this hints to us *the exceeding freeness of His delightfulness*.

I. First, then, the text sets forth THE EXCEEDING DELIGHTFULNESS OF OUR LORD.

He compares Himself here, not as in other places, to *necessary* bread and refreshing water, but to lovely flowers, to roses and lilies. What is the use of roses and lilies? I know what the use of corn is—I must eat it—it is necessary to me for food. I know why barley and rye and all sorts of roots and fruits are created—they are the necessary food of man or beast. But what do we need with roses? What do we need with lilies? They are of no use at all except for joy and delight. With their sweet form, their charming color and their delicious fragrance, we are comforted and pleased and delighted, but they are not necessaries of life. A man can live without roses—there are millions of people, I have no doubt—who live without possessing lilies of the valley. There are all too few roses and lilies in this smoky Babylon of ours, but, when we do get them, what are their uses? Why, they are things of beauty, if not "a joy forever!"

Jesus is all that and more! He is far more than "a thing of beauty" and, to all who trust Him, He will be "a joy forever." To you who are Christ's people, He is your bread, for you feed on Him and He makes you live! You could not do without Him as the sustenance of your soul. He is the Living Water and your soul would pine and perish of a burning thirst if you did not drink of Him! But that is not all that Jesus is to you—God has never intended to save His people on the scale of the workhouse—to give you just as much as you absolutely need, and nothing more. No, no, no! He means you to have *joy* as well as to have *life*. To look upon beauty as well as to be in safety and to have not only a healthy atmosphere, but an atmosphere that is laden with the odor of sweet flowers! You are to find in Christ roses and lilies, as well as bread and water! You have not yet *seen* all His beauties and you do not yet *know* all His excellence!

The exceeding delightfulness of Christ is suggested to our mind by His declaration, "I am the rose, and I am the lily." And first, *He is, in Himself, the delight of men*. He speaks not of offices, gifts, works, possession—but of Himself—"I Am." Our Lord Jesus is the best of all beings! The dearest, sweetest, fairest and most charming of all beings that we can think of is the Son of God, our Savior! Come here, you poets who dream of beauty, and then try to sing its praises—but your imagination could never reach up to the matchless perfection of His Person—neither could your sweetest music ever attain to the full measure of His praise! Think of Him as the God-Man, God Incarnate in human nature and absolutely perfect! I was going to say something more than that, for there is not only in Him all that there ought to be, but there is more than your thoughts or wishes have ever compassed! Eyes need to be trained to see beauty. No man sees half or a *thousandth* part of the beauty, even, of this poor, natural world. But the painter's eyes—the eyes of Turner, for instance—can see much more than you or I ever saw.

"Oh," said one, when he looked on one of Turner's landscapes, "I have seen that view every day, but I never saw as much as *that* in it." "No," replied Turner, "don't you wish you could?" And, when the Spirit of God trains and tutors the eyes, they see in Christ what they never saw before. But, even then, as Turner's eyes were not able to see all the mystery of God's beauty in nature, so neither is the most trained and educated Christian able to perceive all the matchless beauty that there is in Christ!

I do not think, Brothers and Sisters, that there is anything about Christ but what should make His people glad. There are dark Truths of God concerning Him, such as His bearing our sin, but what a joy it is to us that He did bear it and put it away forever! It makes us weep to look at Jesus dying on the Cross, but there is more real joy in the tears of *repentance* than there is in the smiles of worldly mirth. I would choose my Heaven to be a Heaven of everlasting weeping for sin sooner than have a Heaven—if such a Heaven could be—consisting of perpetual laughing at the mirth of fools! There is more true pleasure in mourning before God than in dancing before the Devil! Christ is, then, all beauty—even the dark parts in Him are the Light of God—and the bitter parts are sweet. He has only to be seen by you and you must perceive whether it is His Godhead or His Manhood; whether it is His priesthood, His royalty, or His prophetic office; whether it is on the Cross or on the Throne; whether it is on earth, or in Heaven, or in the Glory of His Second Coming, every way—

"All over glorious is my Lord,
Must be beloved, and yet adored.
His worth, if all the nations knew,
Sure the whole earth would love Him too."

But, next, our Lord is *exceedingly delightful to the eyes of faith*. He not only tells us of what delight is in Himself—"I am the rose, and I am the lily"—but He thereby tells us that there is something to see in Him, for the rose is very pleasing to look upon. Is there a more beautiful sight than a rose that is in bud, or even one that is full blown? And the lily—what a charming thing it is! It seems to be more a flower of Heaven than of earth! Well now, Christ is delightful to the eyes of faith. I remember the first time I ever saw Him—I shall never forget that sight—and, by His Grace, I have seen Him many times since, but my grief is that I ever take my eyes off Him, for it is to look away from the sun into blackness! It is to look away from bliss into misery! To you who look at Christ by faith, a sight of Him brings such peace, such rest, such hope, as no other sight can ever afford—it so sweetens everything, so entirely takes away the bitterness of life and brings us to anticipate the glory of the life that is to come, that I am sure you say—"Yes, yes, the figure in the text is quite correct, there is a beauty in Jesus to the eyes of faith! He is, indeed, red as the rose and white as the lily."

And, next, the Lord Jesus Christ is *delightful in the savor which comes from Him to us*. In Him is a delicious, varied, abiding fragrance which is very delightful to the spiritual nostril. Smell is, I suppose, a kind of delicate feeling—minute particles of certain substances touch sensitive membranes—and we call the sensation that is produced, *smelling*. It is a mysterious sense. You can understand sight and hearing better than you can understand smelling. There is a spiritual way of perceiving the savor of Christ—I cannot explain it to you, but there is an ineffable mysterious sweetness that proceeds from Him which touches the spiritual senses and affords supreme delight—and as the body has its nose, and its tender nerves that can appreciate sweet odors, so the soul has its spiritual nostril by which, though Christ is at a distance, it yet can perceive the fragrant emanations that come from Him and is delighted therewith!

What is there that comes from Christ, from day to day, but His Truth, His Spirit, His influence, His promises, His doctrines, His words of cheer? All these have a heavenly sweetness and make us, with the Psalmist, say to our Lord, "All Your garments smell of myrrh, and aloes, and cassia out of the ivory palaces, whereby they have made You glad." Whenever these sweet odors are wafted down to us, they also make us glad—anything that has the savor of Christ in it is sweet to a Christian! If Christ has touched it, let me put it in my bosom and keep it there as a sweet forget-me-not until I see His face in Glory! Yes, the very stones He sat on—I was about to say the very mountains at which He *looked*—have become dear to us! We have no idolatrous or superstitious reverence for Palestine, or even for the garden in which He sweat great drops of blood, but for *spiritual* things with which He has to do, we have a never-ceasing reverence and affection. Everything that comes from Him is wondrous as the songs of angels must have been to the shepherds of Bethlehem—and sweet to the taste as the manna that dropped from the skies around Israel's desert camp. Yes, Brothers and Sisters, there is a sweet savor about the Lord Jesus Christ! Do you all perceive it?

Once more, *in all that He is, Christ is the choicest of the choice.* You notice the Bridegroom says, "I am the rose." Yes, but there were some particularly beautiful roses that grew in the valley of Sharon. "I am that rose," He said. And there were some delightful lilies in Palestine—it is a land of lilies! There are so many of them that nobody knows which lily Christ meant and it does not at all tell us, for almost all lilies are wondrously beautiful. "But," He said, "I am the lily of the valleys." The choicest kind of lily grew where the soil was fat and damp with the overflow of mountain streams. "I am the lily of the valleys," that is to say, Christ is not only good, but He is the best! And He is not only the best, but He is the best of the best! He is a flower—yes, but He is a rose, the queen of flowers—yes, but then He is the best rose there is, He is the rose of Sharon! He is a Savior, and a great one. Yes, the *only* Savior. He is a Husband, but what a Husband! Was there ever such a Bridegroom as Christ Jesus the Lord? He is the Head, but father Adam was a poor head compared with Him! He is inexpressibly, unutterably, indescribably lovely! I might as well leave off talking about Him, for I cannot hope to set Him forth as He deserves! If you could but see Him, I would leave off, for I am sure I should be only hanging a veil before Him with the choicest words that I could possibly use!

Suppose you had a dear son, or husband, or friend, far away, and that I was a painter who could carry pictures in my mind's eye, and then draw them to the very life. If I stood here, trying to paint your well-beloved friend, laying on my colors with all the skill I possessed and doing my best to reproduce his features, suppose, while I was at work, that the door at the back was opened and he came in? I would cry out, "Oh, stop, stop, stop! Let me put away my canvas, let me pack up my brushes and my paints. Here is the loved one, himself—look at him! Look at *him*, not at my portrait of him!" And you would rise from your seat and say, "It is he! It is he! You may talk as long as you like, dear Sir, when he is away, but when he is, himself, here, your talk seems but mere chatter." Well, I shall be quite content that you should think so, I shall be even glad if you do, provided that the reason shall be that you can say, "We have seen the Lord. He has manifested Himself to us as He does not to the world." "I am the rose of Sharon, and the lily of the valleys." The best of the best, the fairest of the fair, and the sweetest of the sweet is Jesus Christ to you and to me if we are, indeed, His people. I cannot say more about the exceeding delightfulness of my Lord. I wish I could.

II. I must pass on, next, to notice THE SWEET VARIETY OF CHRIST'S DELIGHTFULNESS.

He is not only full of joy, pleasure and delight to our hearts, but He is full of all sorts of joy, and all sorts of pleasure, and all sorts of delights to us—

> *"Nature, to make her beauties known,*
> *Must mingle colors not her own."*

The rose is not enough. You must also have the lily, and the two together fall far short of the glories of Christ, the true, "Plant of renown."

"I am the rose." That is *the emblem of majesty*. The rose is the very queen of flowers. In the judgment of all who know what to admire, it is enthroned above all the rest of the beauties of the garden. But the lily—what is that? That is *the emblem of love*. The Psalmist hints at this in the title of the 45th Psalm. "Upon Shoshannim, a Song of Love." Shoshannim signifies lilies, so the Lily Psalm is the love song for the lilies, with their beauty, their purity, their delicacy, are a very choice emblem of love! Are you not delighted when you put these two things together, majesty and love? A King upon a throne of love! A Prince, whose very eyes beam with love to those who put their trust in Him, a real Head, united by living bonds of love to all His members—such is our dear Lord and Savior! A rose and yet a lily. I do not know in which of the two I take the greater delight—I prefer to have the two together. When I think that my Savior is King of kings and Lord of lords, I shout, "Hallelujah!" But when I remember that He loved me and gave Himself for me and that He still loves me, and that He will keep on loving me forever and ever, there is such a charm in this thought that nothing can excel it! Look at the lily and sing—

> *"Jesus, lover of my soul,*
> *Let me to Your bosom fly,*
> *While the nearer waters roll,*
> *While the tempest still is high!*
> *Hide me, O my Savior, hide,*
> *Till the storm of life are past.*
> *Safe into the haven guide*
> *Oh receive my soul at last!*

Then look at the rose and sing—

> *"All hail the power of Jesus' name!*
> *Let angels prostrate fall.*
> *Bring forth the royal diadem,*
> *And crown Him Lord of All!"*

Then put the rose and the lily together and let them remind you of Christ's majesty and love. The combination of these sweet flowers also suggests our Lord's *suffering and purity*—

> **"White is His soul, from blemish free.**
> **Red with the blood He shed for me."**

The rose, with its thorn, reminds us of His suffering, His bleeding love to us, His death on our behalf, His bearing of the thorns which our sin created. Christ is a royal rose beset with thorns, but the lily shows that—

> **"For sins not His own**
> **He died to atone."**

Jesus, when on earth, could say, "The prince of this world comes, and has nothing on Me." The Devil himself could not see a spot or speck in that lovely lily! Jesus Christ is perfection itself! He is all purity, so you must put the two together, the rose and the lily, to show Christ's suffering and perfection, the infinitely pure, infinitely suffering. In which of the two do you take the greater delight? Surely, in neither, but in the combination of both! What would be the value of Christ's sufferings if He were not perfect? And of what use would His perfections be if He had not died, the Just for the unjust, to bring us to God? But the two together, the rose and the lily, suffering and purity, fill us with delight!

Of both of these there is a great variety. I wonder how many different sorts of roses there are? I would not like to have to tell you! They vary exceedingly—perhaps there are as many kinds as there are days in the year. How many varieties of lilies are there? Possibly, there are as many sorts of lilies as there are of roses, for both of them are wonderfully diversified, but the joys that flow from our Lord Jesus Christ are as abundant and as varied as the roses and the lilies together! Bring me which rose you please and I will tell you that it smells sweet. Bring which lily you choose, and I will say, "Yes, that, also, has a delicate perfume. That will do, *with the rose*, to serve as an emblem of Christ." Our Lord Jesus possesses every kind of beauty and fragrance. "He is all my salvation and all my desire." All good things meet in Christ—in Him all the lines of beauty are focused! Blessed are they who truly know Him.

Further, *Christ is the very essence of the sweetness, both of the rose and of the lily.* When He says, "I am the rose," He means not only that He is like the rose, but that He *made* all the sweetness there is in the rose—and it is still in Him! And all the sweetness there is in *any* creature comes to us from Christ, or else it is not sweetness such as we ought to love. I like to look upon the bread I eat as His gift to me and to bless His Providential hand that bestows it. I like to look upon all the landscape on such a fair day as this has been, and say, "Christ is in all this, giving this charming view to such a poor, unworthy creature as I am." He is in all there is that is good! He is the goodness of all the good there is! He is the very soul of the universe, whatever there is in the universe that is worthy of our soul's love! All good for our soul comes from Him, whether it is pardon of sin, or justification, or the sanctification that makes us fit for Glory hereafter, Christ is the Source of it all and in the infinite variety of delights that we get from Him, He is, Himself, the essence of it all.

We can become tired of most things. I suppose that we can become tired of everything *earthly*. But we shall never tire of Christ! I remember one who, when near his death hour, forgot even his wife, and she was greatly grieved that he did not recognize her. They whispered in his ear the name of his favorite child, but he shook his head. His oldest friend, who had known him from his boyhood, was not recognized. At last they asked him, "Do you know Jesus Christ?" Then he said, "Ah, yes, and by His Grace I am going to Him!" The ruling passion was strong in death—Christ was nearer and dearer to him than those he loved best on earth! All flowers will fade, even roses and lilies among them, but not this blessed Rose of Sharon and Lily of the valleys!

Christ does not say, "I *was* a rose and I *was* a lily," but, "I *am* the rose, and I *am* the lily." He is now all that He ever was! And He will be—in life, in death and throughout all eternity to the soul that knows Him—an infinite variety of everything that is delightful!

III. I must now, very briefly, take up the last head of my discourse which is THE EXCEEDING FREENESS OF OUR LORD'S DELIGHTFULNESS.

It is not very pleasant or satisfying for hungry people to stand in the street and hear someone praising a good meal of which they cannot even get a taste. I have often noticed boys standing outside a shop window in which there have been all sorts of dainties—they have flattened their noses against the window—but they have not been able to get anything to eat.

I have been talking about my Master and I want to show you that *He is accessible*, He is meant to be plucked and enjoyed as roses and lilies are! He says in the text, "I am the rose of Sharon." What was Sharon? It was an open plain where anybody might wander and where even cattle roamed at their own sweet will. Jesus is not like a rose in Solomon's garden, shut up within high walls with broken glass all along the top. Oh, no! He says, "I am the rose of Sharon," *everybody's* rose, the flower for the common people to come and gather. "I am the lily." What lily? The lily of the palace of Shushan, enclosed and guarded from all approach? No, but "I am the lily of the valleys," found in this glen, or the other ravine, growing here, there and everywhere! "I am the lily of the valleys."

Then *Christ is as abundant as a common flower.* Whatever kind of rose it was, it was a common rose.

Whatever kind of lily it was, it was a well-known lily that grew freely in the valleys of that land. Oh, blessed be my Master's name, He has brought us a common salvation and He is the common people's Christ! Men in general do not love Him enough, or else they would have hedged Him in with all sorts of restrictions—they would have made a franchise for Him and nobody would have been able to be saved except those who paid, I know not how much a year in taxes! But they do not love our Lord enough to shut Him in and I am glad they have never tried to do so. There He stands, at the four Cross roads, so that everybody who comes by and wants Him, may have Him! He is a Fountain bearing this inscription, "Let him that is thirsty, come. And whoever will, let him take of the Water of Life freely."

"I am the rose of Sharon, and the lily of the valleys." Why do roses grow in Sharon? Why do lilies grow in the valleys? Why, to be plucked, of course! I like to see the children go down into the meadow when it is decked in grass and adorned with flowers—gilded with buttercups, or white with the daisies! I love to see the children pluck the flowers and fill their aprons with them, or make garlands and twist them round their necks, or put them on their heads. "O children, children!" somebody might cry, "do not spoil those beautiful flowers, do not go and pick them." Oh, but they may! Nobody says they may not—they may not go into our *gardens* and steal the geraniums and the fuchsias—but they may get away into the meadows, or into the open fields and pluck these common flowers to their heart's content! And now, poor Soul, if you would like an apron full of roses, come and have them! If you would like to carry away a big handful of the lilies of the valleys, come and take them—as many as you will! May the Lord give you the will! That is, after all, what is needed. If there is that Grace-given will, the Rose of Sharon and the Lily of the valleys will soon be yours! They are common flowers, growing in a common place, and there are plenty of them—will you not take them?

Even to those who do not pluck any, there is one strange thing that must not be forgotten. A man passes by a rose bush, and says, "I cannot stop to think about roses," but as he goes along, he exclaims, "Dear, dear, what a delicious perfume!" A man journeying in the east goes through a field that is full of lilies. He is in a great hurry, but, for all that, he cannot help seeing and smelling the lilies as he rushes through the field. And, do you know, the perfume of Christ has life in it? He is "a savor of life to life." What does that mean but that the smell of Him will save? Ah, if you do but glance at Him, though you were so busy that you could not come in till the sermon had begun, yet a glance at this Lily will bring you joy and peace, for He is so free that, often, even when men are not asking for Him, He comes to them!

"What?" you say, "is it really so?" Yes, that it is! Such is the freeness of Christ's Grace that it is written, "I am found of them that sought Me not." He sends His sweet perfume into nostrils that never sniffed after it. He puts Himself in the way of eyes that never looked for Him! How I wish that some man who has never sought for Christ might find Him even now! You remember the story that Christ tells of the man that was plowing the field? He was only thinking of the field and how much corn it would take to sow it. He was plowing up and down, when suddenly his plowshare hit upon something hard. He stopped the oxen and took his spade, and dug, and there was an old crock full of gold! Somebody had hidden it away and left it. This man had never looked for it, for he did not even know it was there, but he had stumbled on it, as men say, by *accident*. What did he do? He did not tell anybody, but he went off to the man who was the owner of the field and said, "What will you take for that field?" "Can you buy it?" "Yes, I want it. What will you take for it?"

The price was so high that he had to sell the house he lived in, his oxen and his very clothes off his back, but he did not care about that! He bought the field and he bought the treasure. And then he was able to buy back his clothes, his house, his oxen and everything else. If you find Christ and if you have to sell the coat off your back in order to get Him; if you have to give up everything you have that you may find Him, you will have such a treasure in Him that, for the joy of finding

Him, you would count all the riches of Egypt to be less than nothing and vanity!

But you need not sell the coat off your back—Christ is to be had for nothing—only you must give Him yourself. If He gives Himself to you and He becomes your Savior, you must give yourself to Him and become His servant. Trust Him, I beseech you! The Lord help you to do so, for Jesus' sake! Amen.

ABOUT THE AUTHOR

Charles Haddon (C. H.) Spurgeon, was born on June 19, 1834, in Kelvedon, Essex, and died on January 31, 1892. He started preaching when he was 15. He married Susannah Thompson in 1856, and their twin sons, Thomas and Charles, were born on September 20, 1857.

He has been called the "Prince of Preachers," and his sermons are among the best in Christian literature.

Printed in Great Britain
by Amazon